KU-064-336

SONGS
OF MY
LIFE

...Slightly Out of Tune

ALSO BY SUSAN DINTINO

Books

A Year of Me

CDs

*Butterfly Blessings: A Healing Meditation
& Invocation of the Archangels*

SONGS
OF MY
LIFE
...Slightly Out of Tune

Susan Dintino

INSIGHTS

HAY HOUSE, INC.

Carlsbad, California • New York City
London • Sydney • Johannesburg
Vancouver • Hong Kong • New Delhi

Copyright © 2012 by Susan Dintino

Published and distributed in the United States by: Hay House, Inc.: www.hayhouse
.com® • *Published and distributed in Australia by:* Hay House Australia Pty. Ltd.:
www.hayhouse.com.au • *Published and distributed in the United Kingdom by:*
Hay House UK, Ltd.: www.hayhouse.co.uk • *Published and distributed in the
Republic of South Africa by:* Hay House SA (Pty), Ltd.: www.hayhouse.co.za •
Distributed in Canada by: Raincoast: www.raincoast.com • *Published in India
by:* Hay House Publishers India: www.hayhouse.co.in

Cover design: Amy Rose Grigoriou • *Interior design:* Nick C. Welch

All rights reserved. No part of this book may be reproduced by any mechanical,
photographic, or electronic process, or in the form of a phonographic recording;
nor may it be stored in a retrieval system, transmitted, or otherwise be copied for
public or private use—other than for "fair use" as brief quotations embodied in
articles and reviews—without prior written permission of the publisher.

The author of this book does not dispense medical advice or prescribe the
use of any technique as a form of treatment for physical, emotional, or medical
problems without the advice of a physician, either directly or indirectly. The
intent of the author is only to offer information of a general nature to help you
in your quest for emotional and spiritual well-being. In the event you use any of
the information in this book for yourself, which is your constitutional right, the
author and the publisher assume no responsibility for your actions.

Library of Congress Control Number: 2011934888

Tradepaper ISBN: 978-1-4019-3802-4
Digital ISBN: 978-1-4019-3803-1

Printed in the United States of America

This book is dedicated to my brother, Tom, who lived his life with strength, courage, and dignity.

CONTENTS:
My Playlist

Introduction

A funny thing happened to me on the way to this moment in my life—I was reminded of a fantasy I've had since I was a little girl. All I wanted to do was make a difference while making someone laugh. I'm not a stand-up comedian or the proverbial life of the party. Heck, I wasn't even the class clown. But I have always delighted in sharing a well-put phrase that brings about a smile that turns into a chuckle and then a good, old-fashioned belly laugh.

Nothing lightens the soul like laughter. That's the reason why I wrote this book. I wanted to share a chuckle or two while mulling over life's biggest challenges, including family, love, marriage, aging parents, and finding our true passion in this crazy world. I wanted to do this through humor and provide some light on those days when the laughter comes easy and also on those days when it's a challenge to even crack a smile.

I believe we're all on this crazy journey together and the only thing better than laughing—or just about as good—is music. That's why I've combined those two loves and dubbed my stories, the melodies I'm sharing with you: *Songs of My Life . . . Slightly Out of Tune.*

What you read will, I hope, fill you with joy and inspire moments of reflection and a few tears. Perhaps you'll find your own song or a refrain that seems familiar. And it's my desire that you find *aha* moments that make you want to sing out loud. After all, we all have our own songs to sing, and they're all equally beautiful, even if they're slightly—or completely—out of tune. To hell with judgment.

Sing. Laugh. Love.

And please join me for the first chorus of the *Songs of My Life*.

❖ ❖ ❖

CHAPTER 1

Just the Way You Are

I've been up and down the numbers on my bathroom scale so many times that I think I've lost and regained a small African country. This means I have clothes in my closet that could fit my seven-year-old granddaughter and others that could house that small African country.

I've had a "weight challenge" for as long as I can remember, and I think that's a great politically correct term for it. It all began when my figure started to blossom and I acquired a hated neighborhood nickname, "Chubza," a not-so-kind play on my maiden name, Kobza. My parents took to kindly asking me if I really needed to eat that bowl of ice cream, and I began to think that food was my enemy. How could I not feel ugly, homely, and like an unwanted fat person? Looking back, I realize that this is where my problems originated when it comes to my weight.

The good news is that I'm the greatest dieter in the world. I've eaten eggs, eggs, *and more eggs* on a diet that I was assured the U.S. ski team used and that would have made even the late Dr. Atkins grimace. Like Rocky Balboa preparing for his battle with Apollo Creed, I was vigilant with my egg intake. Although, fearing salmonella, I did cook them—no fool here. I've made soups that eat away fat and drunk drinks that gave me more pep than what drives Robin Williams on a slow day. I've kept food journals, exercise schedules, and attended motivational meetings . . . all to no avail.

I lost, oh yes, I lost, but I soon put it all back on, plus a few pounds more for good measure. Sadly, I became a statistic, one of the millions who lose weight only to gain it back. I asked myself what motivated me to put myself through these dietary acrobatics. Was I a closet masochist? Did I just love eggs?

Deep down, I knew the answer pure and simple. Every time I looked at myself in the mirror, a fat woman looked back at me. I yelled at her, demeaned her, and said things to her that I'd never say to my worst enemy. When these bouts of self-abuse kicked in, I turned to my best friends, who lived in the fridge and pantry. Nothing soothed my soul like a hot-fudge sundae and a box of Oreo cookies. But even with these sweet binges, I realized the problem wasn't what I was eating; it truly was what was eating me.

THIS SHIFT IN PERCEPTION BEGAN when I turned 40. My husband had a surprise birthday party for me, and one of my good friends had lovingly put together a scrapbook of photos of me, past and present. Looking through it, I realized that I never really was *that* overweight; it was just my opinion of that woman in the pictures. I didn't like her very much, let alone love her. I understood that rather than changing my body, I had to figure out how to like myself just the way I was. I had to learn to afford myself the same kindness I gave to others.

How in the world was I going to do this? The answer was I had to start slowly.

I'd been reading quite a few metaphysical books at the time, and their overwhelming consensus was that words have an enormous amount of power. I knew that my self-talk was less than flattering, to say the least, and the first step I had to take was to stop the verbal abuse I heaped on myself whenever I saw my reflection, especially in a full-length mirror. I was a master at catching glimpses of myself in store windows and mirrors and quickly looking away. I acted as if seeing that woman could turn me into a fat person I didn't want to be, much the way Medusa could turn people to stone. I knew that had to change, so I came up with a plan. Every time I looked in the mirror and felt ready to say something nasty to myself, I stopped, took a deep breath, and thought of something positive instead. I wouldn't allow the negative thoughts to be voiced in my head, let alone come out of my mouth.

I started to look at myself and smile . . . just smile. This was my first step to self-acceptance. After this started getting easier, I decided to perceive myself in a new light. I wanted to concentrate on the positive parts of my physical appearance. Instead of telling myself, *You're so fat!* I smiled and thought, *You have beautiful eyes!*

2

I allowed myself to experience how it really felt to receive a compliment. The key was that I not only said the words, but also experienced the emotion that went along with them. In order to change—really change—I knew that I had to transform the way I felt about myself, not just use different words.

Complimenting yourself may feel unnatural and even silly, but believe me, it works. It transforms the way you feel about yourself and ultimately the way you actually see yourself. One of the benefits of viewing yourself in a positive light is that it's easier to accept compliments.

I was the type of person who had a real problem graciously accepting anything nice that people said about me because I always distrusted their motives, thinking, *Were they just being kind? What do they want now? They can't possibly mean that I look great. Do their glasses need an adjustment? If only they knew what I weighed.* I never felt that I deserved positive feedback that pertained to my appearance. I never believed they were truthful.

This realization came as a bit of a shock to me. In my quest for self-acceptance, I knew that I had to accept compliments gracefully and completely—really receive them. When someone flattered me, I had to come up with a positive response instead of turning around to see who they were really talking to, thinking it couldn't possibly be me. Again, I started slowly, proceeding with caution.

When someone said something nice to me, I could feel the "Thank you, but . . ." starting to come out of my mouth, but caught myself and simply said, "Thank you." Just those two magic words . . . *thank you* . . . no buts allowed. At first it was a challenge. No one has ever accused me of being short on words; but I found that the more I practiced it, the easier it became. I'm to the point now that if I get my hair done and my husband doesn't compliment me on how fabulous I look, he's the one who has to come up with some buts!

This part of my path to self-acceptance has been a joyous journey—not necessarily a short one, but well worth the time it took to travel. I learned a great deal along the way and am proud of the woman I am now. Regardless of where the numbers are on the scale,

I know that my beauty shines from the inside out. Before getting to this point, however, there were still more obstacles ahead.

PICTURES OF MYSELF WERE ANOTHER MAJOR stumbling block I had to overcome before arriving at this point. I was the only one in the house whose portrait wasn't prominently displayed. My daughters teased me that if anything happened and they needed a photo of me, they'd have to use my driver's license photo. Heaven forbid! The image on my ID looks like Nick Nolte's mug shot. Talk about a bad-hair day. I hated having my picture taken because I despised the way I looked, and I wasn't about to get into the frame if I could help it.

I was a master at avoiding photos at all costs, at all functions, even feigning a weak bladder or pink eye. I'd do anything to avoid the camera. When all else failed, I volunteered to take the picture. I exuded the professionalism of Annie Leibovitz behind the lens, although I certainly didn't have her talent. If I couldn't escape that way, I always positioned myself so that I was barely visible at all. I usually looked like no more than a floating head with a toothy smile, similar to the Cheshire cat in *Alice in Wonderland*. When my family looked at all those pictures, they asked where I was or practically needed a magnifying glass to find me. After one particularly grueling day spent avoiding the dreaded photographer at a cousin's wedding, where I almost fell into the cake trying to escape, I knew this had to stop. If I was truly on the road to self-acceptance, I had to overcome my phobia.

Christmas was coming up, and it was the perfect time to take the plunge. I decided to give my family a professional portrait of myself. Just the thought of it brought me to the verge of panic, but I wouldn't be deterred. I decided that if I was going to do this, I was going to do it right, so I planned a visit to my favorite salon to get my hair and makeup done for the session.

As I walked in the door of the photographer's studio, I left all my inhibitions behind. In that time and place, I was no longer Susan but instead an international supermodel. Heidi Klum, eat your heart out. I'd handpicked every outfit and gone for brilliant colors that flattered my complexion versus the old "What makes me look thin?" trap that I usually fell into. I preened and strutted my stuff the entire time and enjoyed every minute of it. I couldn't wait for the pictures to come.

When the proofs arrived, I ripped open the envelope and spread them all out on the kitchen table. I was excited, but as I looked at each one, I felt my enthusiasm fade. Could this be possible? Did I really look *fat* in all of them? I continued to gaze at them; and the more I did, the more I realized that in fact, these pictures were flattering. I looked great. I just wasn't used to seeing myself and, more important, accepting myself. I got excited again and ordered the prints for my family, picking out a special frame for each one of them.

On Christmas morning, I was shaking like a bowl full of jelly when I presented these gifts to my children and my husband. They loved them and thought I looked marvelous. It was the perfect gift, and their reaction actually made me feel like Heidi Klum all over again. The eight-by-ten went up on the mantel with the rest of the family photos, and now every time I look at it, I feel proud and like what I see.

Last year, however, a real test came up. We have a second home on the beach in Florida, where I spend the winter and spring, and it's where the family comes together every year for spring break. It's our favorite place and full of wonderful memories. I decided to celebrate our times there by having a professional family photo taken on the beach. We coordinated our outfits so that we all matched in denim and white. Getting a family of nine to agree on this was no small feat, but I persevered. We had our makeup professionally done, and although the men were in no way in favor of this, they went along with it for my sake. I must admit that they all looked a bit odd, but I wasn't about to say anything. The photographer told me it was necessary, and I took his word for it.

We were doing a sunset photo, and when the time arrived, we all marched down to the shore. The sky was full of the golds, pinks, and purples that only a southwest Florida sky can give you at sundown. Along with this sublime sky was the arrival of what Floridians not so fondly call "no-see-ums." These joyous insects feast on your flesh with bites that itch like a bad pair of Spanx.

Still, we all soldiered on and took many pictures, and I anxiously waited for the proofs. When they came, I frankly did not recognize myself. In case you think I'm exaggerating, my seven-year-old granddaughter saw the picture and asked where Nonni was and who was that blonde lady? There had been so much "touching up" that I was unrecognizable. My husband was thrilled to see that he was married to a blonde bombshell, but I wasn't amused. I called the photographer, and he explained he'd removed my wrinkles and slenderized my figure a bit.

I asked him to send a different proof with me as I am—bumps, wrinkles, and all. I liked it better, and my granddaughter was thrilled to see her Nonni back with the family. My husband, I'm not so sure about. I loved myself, the real me, and thought I looked damn good! The self I loved was surrounded by the things I love the most, including my husband, my family, and that awe-inspiring beach.

Okay, I'd worked on the self-talk and was cool with my picture being taken. The next step in my acceptance process was to look at myself totally naked and not become violently ill. I'm a pretty free spirit where nudity is concerned and am known to walk around the house sans clothing. I know what you're thinking . . . but no, I'm not *that* woman. No one is ever around at these times to see me, nor did I allow myself to ever really look at my reflection. But I figured if I was going to really accept myself, I had to go all the way with it. This was no time for cowardice.

One morning before my shower, I stood fully nude in front of my mirror and did the unthinkable: I looked at myself.

This wasn't just a furtive glance. I really looked. At first, I was horrified. I quickly glanced away and jumped into the shower, hoping that I wouldn't suffer from some type of post-traumatic stress disorder. Then I refocused on the fact that the whole point of this exercise was to show myself kindness. I also reminded myself how fortunate I was to have a healthy body that has served me well. It has always been there when I needed it, and although I'm sure there are times I've let it down, it has never done the same to me. I thought, *This body just as it is right now, right this minute, is a blessing.*

When I got out of the shower, I took another look. It's amazing what a difference my change of attitude had. I noticed my belly and the stretch marks and fondly remembered the three babies that lived there for a time. The breasts that once stood proud had drooped for sure, but I recalled those same babies feeding there and the tenderness of their mouths: *Yes, this body with all of its so-called flaws has served me well.*

With this realization came the first stirrings of total acceptance. I now not only look at my body every day, but I bless it and thank it for all it has done for me.

BEING A BEACH PERSON, A BATHING SUIT is a necessary part of my wardrobe. The last step in my self-acceptance process was to go shopping for this item and not act as if I were getting a tooth pulled. I went to a local store where they brag that they have suits to fit every shape and size, which will turn you into the bathing beauty you've only dreamed of being. I walked in, and the first thing I saw were garments made of string that I knew might have fit me when I was three years old but certainly wouldn't now.

I moved on and looked for things in my size and was pleasantly surprised to see quite a few I liked. One style actually claimed to take ten pounds off your figure. How bad could that be?

I took all my selections into the dressing room and began to try them on. The ten-pound slimmer was quite the challenge to get into. When the saleswoman asked me if I needed assistance, I was tempted to ask her for a crowbar. The only thing I can compare to this experience is trying to get a grapefruit into a shot glass.

When I finally succeeded, I knew why they said I'd look 10 pounds thinner. I think I actually lost that weight getting into it. At first glance, I saw my hair sticking up at all angles and my sunglasses askew. I was sweating profusely from the exertion, but the suit looked good on me. It really did. I could wear this and feel proud of myself. Yay! While I might never wear a thong, I could still strut my stuff.

TODAY, I RELISH WHO I AM and how I look every day. In this time of liposuction, face-lifts, and Botox, I'm happy with what I see

without any toxic enhancements. In contrast, there's currently a popular website by a woman who feels that she's "formerly fabulous," and I feel sad when I think about that. I think that she's 40 now, and there should be no "formerly" about it. She should realize that she's fabulous at any age. I've learned that it's all about accepting yourself just the way you are at this moment.

Don't wait to enjoy the beauty you are. Get your picture taken and choose to like what you see. Accept compliments graciously and honor yourself on a daily basis. Realize the uniqueness of you and how truly wonderful you are. After all, you're one of a kind.

❖ ❖ ❖

CHAPTER 2

Teach Your Children Well

I am the mother of three lovely daughters. My oldest two are now married, and I have three grandchildren. My girls have all brought me a great deal of joy in life; but my youngest, who was gifted with the "free spirit" gene, has truly been a challenge. She lives life as if it's a great adventure. If she were an amusement-park attraction, she would be the roller coaster.

I'm more of a merry-go-round type. She loves the sheer drops and fast dips, while I hold on going two miles an hour on a plastic horse. By the way, Ms. Free Spirit has also taught me the importance of allowing your children to go their way in order to create their own lives and generate their own happiness.

Doesn't all that sound lovely? I must add that I nearly didn't survive this child. Let me tell you a bit about her. . . .

MY YOUNGEST DAUGHTER IS ONE OF THOSE rebound children who's used our home as a pit stop between her many adventures in life. Sometimes she lives with us; sometimes she doesn't. I feel as though our front door is an ever-moving turnstile in her life. When she does live with us due to circumstances such as a sudden loss of employment, I find myself reverting back to being the mom of her teenage years. In those days, it was a rare occasion for me to sleep through the night and not wait up for her. On the nights I wasn't so lucky, I'd wake up, realize she wasn't home yet, and pace the floor as the clock ticked into the wee hours.

Why do I still do this now that she's an adult? I can't tell you. It's just something mothers do because they're still our kids, whether age 10 or 35. Even now that she's in her late 20s, I find the habit hard to break, and my daughter doesn't make it any easier.

SHE'S ALWAYS LIVED on the edge. She didn't give a second thought to the possibility that one day we might both end up on an analyst's couch. Ever since she was a little wild girl, I've assailed her with all kinds of warnings about the peril that might befall a completely unafraid child who had the nerve to stray from her mother's side.

Did this frighten her? Of course not! She took great delight in not only leaving my side, but also playing a great game of hide-and-seek in grocery stores, malls, or playgrounds. Even in our neighborhood, she thought nothing of venturing out of the backyard at the age of three to take a stroll around the block—solo!

After a few minutes of frantic searching, I found her and then demanded why she'd walked around the block. My daughter simply said, "Because it was there."

From that point on, I knew I was in for a long haul with this child.

Once, I had the idea of offering to lend her to Third World countries as a form of birth control, believing that anyone who had to spend any time rearing this girl would quickly abstain from doing anything that could put them in a position where they might have one of their own. There were no takers. Her passport was put away.

I GET HIVES LOOKING BACK TO THE TIME she was a senior in high school. She had senioritis from the first day of school in September, and by June, it was full blown. She went out every single night, including Tuesdays *when no one goes out*. I couldn't figure out how she did it. I was *never* that young. If I questioned her, she got this puzzled look on her face, tilted her head, and looked as if I were speaking a language she didn't quite understand. All her friends went out every night. Didn't I know that? That's just the way it was.

She was 17 and had a better social life than Michelle Obama and Kim Kardashian rolled into one. You might ask, where did she go? Wherever she wanted, I'd answer. The bars were no obstacles, despite her underage status. Her driver's license had been altered so many times that I don't think she knew what year she was born in any longer.

I know, I know. You're probably thinking, *How did this child get so out of control? Is this woman just the most permissive parent around?*

I've asked myself the same question. The thing is that if I am that mom, then I know I'm not alone. All her friends were there, too; and whether they lied or told their parents the truth, they were still joining her on her nightly escapades. Maybe the entire class had permissive parents.

There's the "Wait until your father gets home" theory of parenting a free spirit. That sounded good, but my husband had just given up. Whenever I complained about her as a teen, he shrugged and said that she "could be worse." Knowing what a night owl my husband was in his youth and can still be at times, I'm convinced it's something in the genes.

I'LL NEVER FORGET THE WEEK WHEN she'd really outdone herself. She was a lifeguard, which was one of those cool summer jobs for a child who always seemed to have fun employment tossed her way. Still, I'd seen these gigs come and go. Her résumé at this point in high school was already two pages long. She always started a new job with great enthusiasm, but being the type of person she is, things could never live up to her expectations. The perfect fit would be something where she got paid lots of money, had a great time, and most important, could fit the drudgery into her ever-changing social calendar. This lifeguarding was just what she wanted because it combined pay with tanning and socializing.

Of course, no new venture came on the horizon that didn't cost Mom and Dad some cash. She needed to take a course to learn how to be a lifeguard, so we gladly shelled out the $125, feeling that it was a worthwhile investment. Tanning being the great motivator, she passed the class with flying colors.

The next step was to get hired. Naturally, all the jobs that were located a reasonable distance from our house required some experience while she had none. Not to be undone, she finally found a position approximately 30 minutes away. This may not seem like much, but my daughter had a hard time getting to school on time, and that was only five minutes away. I knew this was going to be trouble.

The first week went well, and she came home looking tanned and rested. The little ones were still in school, and she didn't have much

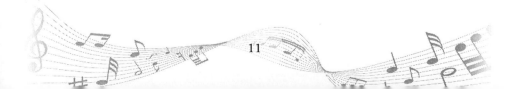

to do. By the third week, however, I noticed that she was becoming very interested in the weather. She wasn't looking for the sun, but instead was hoping for showers. Everyone was out of school, and her work had started in earnest. It required actual *lifeguarding*—of all the dirty tricks. Her only out was when it rained.

I pointed out that the season had just begun, and I couldn't believe she was already scanning the sky for thunderheads. She looked at me with great exasperation, grabbed the clicker, settled on the Weather Channel, and refused to answer.

Week 4 marked car trouble. Her ride needed to be reliable because her job required travel time. This fact was presented at the family dinner table in a tone that was so serious, we might have thought she was driving to North Carolina to save lives.

"I have to take Mom's car because you don't want me to get stranded on the road and get murdered," she said, trying to instill parental fear. This child knew how to push buttons, and discussing her own demise did the job.

With great wisdom and clutching his own car keys for dear life, my husband agreed with her. Of course, I fell right into the guilt thing and agreed to give up my car. The weather was nice, and I could ride my bike to do the few errands I had. They both assured me that this would only be for one or two days, so why worry? Meanwhile, the working girl's car was taken to the mechanic, and the next day my husband called with the prognosis.

"Do you want the good news or the bad news first?" he joked.

I'd just completed my first bike errand, which had involved balancing a giant roll of wrapping paper in a two-by-two wire basket, which was also filled with a gallon of milk and a dozen eggs. I rode like Julie Andrews in *The Sound of Music* for a mile, but without the singing. In fact, I almost ran head- and gift wrapping–first into the hedges to avoid my neighbors' curious glances.

I wasn't amused as my husband quickly went on.

"They've found the problem with the car," he confidently told me as I waited for the other shoe to drop. "However,"—here it comes—"the parts have to be ordered, so it may be a few more days," he concluded, assuring me that he'd insisted everything be shipped by air so that the wait would be minimal.

Gritting my teeth, I attempted to say a cheery good-bye. What I would have liked to say isn't exactly fit to print.

Instead of cursing, I made myself a cup of tea and decided to relax.

"This will not aggravate me," I whispered as the phone rang again. It was my daughter, calling me from my cellular phone, which was only to be used for emergencies back in those days when the bills were like tiny mortgage payments.

"Hi, Mom!" she said, breathlessly.

"What's up? Why are you calling me?" I asked. "Do you realize this phone is approximately $50 a minute?"

"Chill out!" she answered with great exasperation. "I just wanted to tell you that a cloud moved in, so I closed the pool."

I looked outside, where it was at least 80 degrees with no clouds in sight. She informed me that the weather was different there and that I should respect changing wind systems.

"Are you coming right home? Because I could use the car." I foolishly asked her.

Her answer was rehearsed: "I have a few stops and—oh no!"

"What's the matter?!" I screamed.

It turns out that she'd run (not directly) into the path of a tanker truck and was swerving to avoid an impending collision.

"I didn't crash, but shoot! There's a cop on my tail now," she screamed back. "Oh no! I better go."

I heard the wail of sirens as she hung up.

I couldn't believe it. We'd warned her over and over again about the radar traps on the highway she took to work. I prayed hard, but in my heart, I knew that she'd gotten stopped for speeding.

Again, time seemed to move in slow motion . . . 5 minutes . . . 10 minutes . . . 15 . . . The phone finally rang again with more bad news.

"You're not going to believe this, Mom, but I got a speeding ticket," she griped.

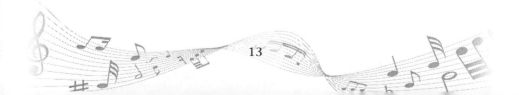

"What a shock," I told her.

Meanwhile, she showed very little remorse, assuring me that the policeman told her that if she went to driving school, the charge would be lessened. My mind became a cash register as I added up how much she'd pay out of her own money for learning her lesson.

"I really need my car," I reminded her again.

"I'll be there soon," she responded.

Knowing "soon" was a relative term in her world, I decided to venture out one more time on the bike. It was a great way to get exercise, I told myself, using my most skeptical inner voice. I was once again balancing the items in my basket like a juggler when who passed me? It was my daughter, talking on my phone and having the nerve to wave to me as she breezed past.

When she got home, she laughed at what she described as the hilarious sight of me on my bike.

Is murder in a case like this really illegal? I wondered.

The next day, my daughter was on her way to her exams, assuring me that my car would be returned the minute she put down her number-two pencil. After the previous day's outing, I decided to stay home and wait.

Two hours late, she ran through our front door and frantically asked me if I'd seen her glasses—*the brand-new ones*. For some reason, her friends thought it was high fashion to wear glasses, especially with designer frames; and my daughter, who will never miss the chance to be a fashionista, *wanted* to wear them.. With college quickly approaching, she assured me that there was no way she'd be an academic success without glasses. As it turned out, she did need them, but she didn't need the $200 designer frames she insisted upon in order to fight off impending death.

I gave in. So sue me. In the scheme of things, I felt this was one of her more reasonable requests. Also, being new to this whole glasses thing, I didn't realize that was an exorbitant amount to pay for frames. These accessories weren't even paid off, and she was telling me that she couldn't find them.

We tracked her movements and finally figured out that she'd left them at a club the night before. Luck was with us, and someone had turned them in. When I told her that she must immediately pick them up, she retorted that it was impossible because she had to work.

Of course, I called the club back. The guy who answered the phone gave me little confidence that those glasses would be there for long. He sounded as if he'd danced one too many times and couldn't be responsible for $200 in social eyewear. I needed a car—I had to get those glasses.

I called my husband, who quickly told me that it was my daughter's problem and I shouldn't be concerned with solving it for her. I informed him that if we didn't get the glasses soon, some party boy named Ben would be wearing them while break-dancing in the streets later that night.

Hanging up, I grabbed my other daughter's keys—the daughter still at home but without the free spirit gene. I knew her car was her prize possession, and it would be easier to get the stripes off of a zebra than convince her to lend it to me, but I was a mother on a mission.

Sensing I had her keys, however, she ran downstairs and asked what I was doing. I haggled with her, promising more than I can admit now, and completed the task.

When I got home, there was a message on the machine from my husband. I called him back, and he informed me that the youngest's car was repaired and ready to be picked up. I couldn't help but smile. Just when you know that you can't possibly stand any more in life, you get a bit of good news. Sure, it was going to cost a fortune, but I didn't care. I smiled because all I could picture was happily sitting in my own car and putting that damn bike into storage.

IN SEPTEMBER OF THAT YEAR, she went away to college—glasses, car, and the rest of her. I made it seem as though it was her choice, but there was no way this kid was staying home for school. I couldn't imagine her with the college freshman know-it-all attitude on top of her adventurous spirit. I would have had to be committed.

When I said good-bye to her in September, there were a few tears because I was facing an empty nest after all. My other daughter who'd been at home was also leaving for law school. (I thought this

profession might really come in handy for her younger sister in the future.) So for what seemed like the first time ever, my husband and I were going to be living alone.

However, I'd instructed my sister that if at any point I bemoaned the fact that I missed my youngest and wished she were home, my sister had my permission to come over and punch me in the face. She told me that she'd gladly do it because even she was sick of hearing my trials and tribulations with this child.

MY OTHER TWO DAUGHTERS WERE relatively low maintenance compared to their sister. They had the traditional growing pains and problems, and we always managed to find a solution. They were what I call normal kids, if there is such a thing. They're both married now and have presented me with the greatest of all inventions . . . grandchildren.

I'm Nonni to these little ones, and I've decided that it would be a wonderful thing if I could have started with grandchildren and then maybe worked my way backward. I get to enjoy them in all their glory, spoil them rotten, and return them to their parents when I'm done. I don't pace the floors waiting for them to come home. It's a beautiful thing, and if it were possible to skip the in-between step of having children first, I'd be the first one in line to vote for it.

What I notice most about my grandchildren is that, although I do fret and worry about them at times, it's not the same pulse-pounding fear I had with my own kids. It's almost as if I feel these children are protected. I think it's mostly because I'm not responsible for them on a daily basis. Nonni is able to truly enjoy all the magic of their childhoods.

ONE OF THE MOST PROFOUND MOMENTS OF MY LIFE was when my oldest daughter gave birth to her son, my first grandchild. I stood outside the delivery room and heard his first wail as he entered the world. Tears filled my eyes as I realized that the child I had brought into the world was now having her own baby. His cry pierced my heart, and I knew that this little boy would be the start of a whole new life—not only his own, but also for me.

On that wonderful day, my son-in-law opened the delivery-room door and invited me in. I saw that tiny baby for the first time, and my daughter handed him to me. The emotions that ran through me as I held him are difficult to describe. We'd waited a long time for a little boy in our family of almost all females.

As I held him, I felt the potential of a new life just as I'd felt when I cradled his mother for the first time. The miracle of it all infused me with an overwhelming joy, and I realized that this is what life is really all about. It's not about the money we earn or the position we hold, but about the lives we bring into the world and their limitless possibilities. Two years later, my daughter gave birth to a little girl, and it was the same joy all over again.

MY SECOND DAUGHTER WAITED A BIT to have children, and when she did get pregnant, I was ready for grandchild number three to be born. When the time came for her to deliver, I was allowed to remain in the waiting room. My daughter had emphatically instructed me that she wanted me to stay there. She didn't want me intruding on that time of hers with her husband, and of course, I respected her wishes.

Would I have preferred being in the labor room, holding her hand, rubbing her back, or doing whatever I could to make her more comfortable? Of course, but I knew that the most important thing was for my daughter to have what she wanted. It wasn't about me and my desires. It was about her.

As I waited, I was sitting across the hall from the nursery. The full moon that night seemed to have done its magic, and there were little newborns everywhere. I don't think I've ever seen so many. It took me back in time to when this daughter was born. It seemed like only yesterday, and here she was having a child of her own. Where did all the time go? I realized it was time to recognize that I'd taught my children well.

AS MY DAUGHTERS AGE, THERE ARE THINGS they do that I agree with and things that I don't. The girls are all kind enough to call and ask me for advice, but then just as determinedly decide not to follow it.

It's been a challenge at points because I was under the delusion that part of being a good mother was keeping my children happy all the time, regardless of their ages. I began to realize as sons-in-law and grandchildren came that even I didn't have the capabilities to always make things okay. Believe me, I tried until I realized it was just plain impossible. It was up to them.

I started my daughters on this journey. I taught them all I could while wiping away their tears, sharing their laughter, and helping solve their problems when I was able to. With new little souls coming into the world, it was time to let them go . . . really let them fly.

These days, I listen to their "venting," as they call it, and realize that it's not a call for my help, let alone my interference. They just want a sympathetic ear, and I can do that. They have their problems and disagreements, and it's not my job to play "mom in the middle," because frankly it just doesn't work. Believe me, I've tried, and all it causes is more problems than it solves. They don't need me to be a mini United Nations.

They're all capable of making their own decisions; and when some of their choices cause them to fall, I realize that these are lessons they're meant to learn. I'm not saying all this newfound wisdom is easy for me, but overall, I can stand back and watch my daughters realizing that they can solve their own problems.

Unless, of course, it's one of those times that I *do* know best. . . .

❖ ❖ ❖

CHAPTER 3

Don't Worry, Be Happy

Birds tweet a merry springtime song as I sit at my laptop with the sun warm on my back and a latte as my companion. This splendor takes place on the porch of my favorite coffeehouse, or my second office. The Bean is located on the main street of my beloved Sanibel Island in southwest Florida. This is a street with no stoplights, where the bicycles at times go faster than the kids racing in Daddy's Corvette or harried mothers driving cautiously in tanklike SUVs. The pace on this island is slow and serene and the landscape totally tropical—the perfect environment for latte sipping.

Does it get any better than this? I ask myself. Then another part of me chimes in and says, *Wait a minute. Shouldn't you be rushing home to take care of all the stuff you have to do—all the things you're responsible for? The list is never ending. How dare you sit sipping a latte when there's laundry to be done and a house to be straightened? What are you going to have for dinner that's nutritious and tasty? Have you lost your mind?"*

With one misplaced thought, my serenity is shattered, and suddenly my latte doesn't taste quite as good, even with the indulgence of some extra whip. How did I go from bliss to bust so fast? Instead of staying in the moment and allowing all my senses to be satiated with the tastes, smells, and sights around me, I propelled myself into a future of to-do lists.

I should be doing this. . . . I should be doing that. . . . Well, I should never have been "shoulding" on myself because what once was bliss is starting to turn into bust, and my enjoyment of the moment threatens to disappear as quickly as my husband does when I ask for his credit card because . . . well, just because. Worries and concerns creep in like an uninvited houseguest and I know if I give in, all serenity will be lost. Luckily, I've learned to turn this tide quickly, but it's never an easy battle to win.

MY NAME IS SUSAN AND I'M A MASTER WORRIER. In fact, I have a Ph.D. in worrying, which, like my brown eyes, I believe was inherited from my darling mother, because even as a child, I worried and she condoned it. I wondered if Santa Claus would like the cookies I left him or if Rudolph would boycott me because naturally he preferred a carrot to an apple. I fretted over whether or not the tooth fairy would really be able to find my tooth under the pillow, so I moved that little sucker so many times I lost track of it. And as I grew older, I discovered something so frightening in my own home that I hate to even bring it up now. Yes, I found my mother's medical books.

Mom was a nurse and had all of these illustrated books of information (read: terror) lying around. One night in college, I couldn't sleep and diagnosed that I was a bit light-headed. Totally freaked out, I raced over to the trusty medical book that I'd "borrowed" from Mom to see what fatal disease I might have contracted. Snakebite from a trip to the Amazon wasn't a possibility, so I crossed that one off the list.

As I looked over the various other diseases, I saw that my condition was one of the symptoms of carbon-monoxide poisoning. I read on, and it said that one could actually get cumulative effects from such things as a leaky car muffler. I had a car! It was old, too, and very possibly had this defective part.

Reading on, I noted that a rash could develop from this toxin entering the system. Suddenly, my left arm began to itch. Wait a minute! Was this a rash I saw or just dry skin? In that moment, my entire body started to prickle.

Luckily, my mother was getting up to go to work at the hospital. Armed with the medical book, I told her that I had to go to the emergency room—stat. Couldn't she take one look at her child and just know that I was suffering from a life-threatening disease? On second glance, Mom thought I'd survive, but I wouldn't be dissuaded. She and my dad begrudgingly took me to the local hospital, only to be told by the doctor that although he didn't normally do this with someone my age, I might need a Valium.

AS I GREW OLDER, IT WAS SO BAD that as soon as my eyes opened in the morning, my first thought was, *What was I worrying about* *before I fell asleep? Oh yes . . . now I remember. My daughter has a slight rash on her leg, which is probably nothing, but what will I do if it spreads over her entire body? Could it be some mysterious jungle fever? Wait, we didn't go to the jungle on vacation, but we did read <u>The Jungle Book.</u> Should I call the doctor? Should I go to the emergency room?* With that, I'd leap out of bed and look up rashes on WebMD, which had replaced my trusty medical encyclopedia.

My relationship with WebMD was not a casual one. I used it so much that it was actually my computer home page. Reading about all the dreaded things the symptom of the day could be, I was in a panic before 8 A.M. and had more adrenaline coursing through me than a purse snatcher on the run. I'm sure you get the picture.

I began to realize that my worrying was becoming so obsessive that it was consuming my life. Everything began innocently enough, but with a few good minutes of thinking, I could bring anything to a worst-case-scenario conclusion. It got so bad that I couldn't truly enjoy anything because I could always find a reason to agonize about something that should have been nothing but a pleasure.

THIS REALLY CAME TO LIGHT FOR ME on a trip I took with my youngest daughter. Her eighth-grade class was traveling to France, and I'd never been to Europe. I was really excited because we were going with an experienced guide, and I could share it with my daughter as well. But . . . there was that creeping dread again. I'd have to fly to get to Europe—a long trip, mostly over water. I'd only flown twice before, and the journeys weren't as long.

As I thought about it more, my mind began to race: *What if the plane had mechanical problems? Where would it land? How could it land? Oh my God! What if the plane goes down?*

As the departure got closer, this worry began to take on a life of its own. The excitement I'd been feeling was replaced with foreboding and dread, and I began to check statistics of plane crashes for 757s made by Boeing in 1980. This was not a good thing.

The day arrived for us to leave, and on my way to the airport, I looked like a condemned woman facing the gallows. I thought I was exuding confidence, but when my daughter saw the look on my

face, she asked me if I was constipated. I knew that I had fooled no one. My husband seemed a bit too relieved. After all, the worrier was going away for 15 days—freedom! He'd heard enough of my disaster "What ifs" and had his fill of my tossing and turning at night. I'm sure he wasn't that sad to see me go. He kissed us hastily and said good-bye.

After we boarded the plane and took off, every muscle in my body was on high alert, waiting for any strange sound. I was wound so tight that even my sphincter was clenched. When the first few hours went well, I began to relax.

I can do this, I thought. *No problem.* Right then, we hit minor turbulence.

Later, after I became a more experienced traveler, I realized that incident was nothing compared to times to come, when the attendants would be seated for almost the entire duration of a flight that was rocking and rolling like we were on a carnival ride. On one of those stormy rides, I actually dropped a Bloody Mary in my husband's lap. Sadly, he was wearing white shorts—but that's a whole other story.

The point is that I can now tell you from experience that these were minor bumps, yet I grabbed my daughter with the grip of a pair of skinny jeans and prepared to get into the crash position. She started laughing hysterically and saw the wide-eyed expressions of her classmates who knew that someone's mom was making an utter fool of herself. As the bumps turned into smooth air, I sheepishly smiled, sat up, and forced myself to relax.

The rest of the flight was uneventful, and when we arrived in Paris it took all my willpower not to kiss the ground like the Pope giving a blessing. I could see the skyline in the distance and actually glimpsed the Eiffel Tower.

Now I can truly enjoy this amazing city, I told myself. That feeling of peace lasted for about a minute and a half.

After a fairly decent night's sleep, we prepared to head to our first destination. All of our travel in France was on a bus. What fun! This was a great way to see the countryside and, best of all, no planes. I just had to get on and enjoy a leisurely drive, watching the scenery gently pass me by.

Then I glanced at the driver and wondered, *How do I know how well this gentleman can drive?*

I'd already noted on the ride from the airport that he didn't believe in deodorant, preferring the eau de cologne of smelly, middle-aged man armpits. The kids had already nicknamed him Smelly Melly.

My mind wandered . . . *If this is the case, what else might he be relaxed about? Braking for sports cars? Roads with sheer drop-offs? What exactly are his credentials?* I knew from what our guide had told us that this trip was going to be taking us through the Alps—up and down winding, narrow roads overlooking steep ravines was on the official schedule of driving joy. One wrong turn and we'd plummet to our deaths. Anxiety once again became my companion. I never allowed my eyes to stray from the driver, and it felt as though my will alone was guiding us through the tough spots.

At one point, I was so focused on how well he was doing that I was actually turning a pretend steering wheel and pumping my foot on an imaginary brake pedal. My daughter was convinced that I'd totally lost my mind and went to sit in the back of the bus as far away from me as she could get. First the plane, and now Mom the bus driver!

When we finally arrived at our destination, everyone was gushing over the beautiful vistas along the way and I realized that I'd missed the whole thing. I hadn't seen the snowcapped majesty of these mountains, the views of the trees, and the wonder of an ever-changing landscape as we rounded each bend in the road. I could tell you with confidence that our driver had a bald spot beginning in the back of his head and a slight case of dandruff, but I couldn't describe the French Alps. I'd missed the glorious experience of driving through one of the most gorgeous, breathtaking wonders of nature.

Our stop was Mont Blanc, the highest summit in the Alps. It was very impressive at 4,807 meters (15,771 feet), and we were making a stop so that we could take a cable car up to the summit, which also happens to hold the distinction of being one of the highest cable cars in the world. You can only imagine the distress I was feeling over that one. The kids and adults poured out of the bus, eagerly getting in line for our adventure. I looked at my daughter and groaned.

"What's the matter now, Mom?" she asked in the slightly annoyed voice that only a teenage girl uses on her parents. As I looked at the height of this mountain and this amusement-park contraption I was expected to board, my bowels began to loosen.

Realizing I couldn't let anyone know my cowardice, however, I powered on. It was eventually our turn, and I got into the cable car, which immediately began to sway—and I began to pray. *Please, I cannot faint dead away in front of all these kids,* I begged God.

The cable car jerked and jolted as we ascended the mountain, and sheer gray rock rose up on both sides. Glancing skyward, I could see the snowcap where we were heading. I looked back and forth between the summer day we were leaving and the winter scenery we were approaching. It seemed impossible to me that the little cabin, literally swinging in the breeze, could possibly take us there.

It's important to note here that I was seated, petrified, with my hands clenched in a death grip. Next to me was a bunch of hyperactive teenagers, and every time they jumped up to see the view on one side of the car, then raced to the other side, the whole rickety thing shifted like the Titanic while hitting that pesky iceberg.

I managed to croak out to them to remember the whole balance thing we'd been warned about. My daughter gave me a look that told me I'd better not say another word. All I could do was close my eyes and wait until the car finally stopped and we got off alive.

The first thing I noticed was how pure the air smelled. It was cold, crisp, and fresh, as though it had never been breathed in by any living thing. *Stunning* could barely describe this location—but it was also freezing. It was hard to believe that I really needed the mittens I had on, when down below I'd been fine in a tank top.

The view of the Alps from this perspective gave me a feeling of a vastness that's difficult to describe. Snowcapped mountaintops in all directions filled my entire range of vision, each one a little bit different but no less beautiful. This was something I wouldn't have wanted to miss. Thank heavens I didn't let my fear win out . . . until . . .

We had an option to go even higher, but I knew my height limits in much the same way that a kid who's short knows that he can't go on every ride at the amusement park. Smiling, I said, "No thanks" to going higher. In about two seconds, I was ditched. Everyone—including the baby I gave birth to after ten hours of horrible labor—ascended, and I was left standing alone in the middle of the Alps.

There was a part of me that was furiously angry—with myself. I knew that I was missing an outstanding, once-in-a-lifetime experience, but I was already stressing about getting back in that swinging thing to get down the mountain. Soon enough, the cable car returned with my group, and I got back in for the return trip, listening to everyone excitedly share what they had seen from a height I was not able to achieve.

I was irate with myself for not going higher. In fact, I was so angry that I actually didn't worry on the trip down, despite the fact that the kids were again making the cable car swing like a Latin dancer's hips. This was the first time anxiety had stopped me from doing something, and I didn't like the experience one bit.

Lying in bed that night, I began to think about how debilitating my constant worrying was becoming. It was sucking the joy out of this trip. I was looking forward to more travel, but how would I ever enjoy it if I let this apprehension have its way with me until I became so phobic that I didn't go anywhere? I'd heard stories of people who became so frightened that they wouldn't leave the house and died with only their cats and clutter around them. That wasn't going to happen to me. For one thing, I didn't have a cat.

Shame on me, I said to myself. The worry addict I knew had to put a stop to this, and right away. Then I had an epiphany: The more I thought about it, the clearer it became that almost everything I worried about never happened. My fretting was all just wasted time when my mind could have been doing something productive. In that moment, in the dark of a French night, I decided to begin to train myself not to worry. When I felt those fearful thoughts creep in, I'd choose a pleasant one to replace it with.

NOW, WHEN I FLY AND the turbulence begins, I tell myself that I'm so grateful that I have the funds for air travel. How great is it that I can get to the places I love quickly and safely? I tell myself, *These are merely the same bumps in the road that a car encounters.* I may also have a few glasses of wine, but one way or another, I don't let the worry win. And I don't need a Valium.

It would be lying to tell you that I never worry anymore—and my family would sure get a kick out of that notion—but I don't let it stop me. I accept it as a part of who I am, but I also have ways to combat it so that it doesn't overpower me. I missed getting to the top of the mountain only once in my life, and it will never happen again.

▦ ▦ ▦

CHAPTER 4

Release Me . . . and My Parents

Not that long ago, I heard someone on television say that we all came from dysfunctional families, so get over it already. I agree with that line of thinking. The Cleaver and Brady clans gave us a skewed perspective of what a "normal" family looked like. Fathers wearing ties to dinner and mothers in dresses while vacuuming was a difficult, if not impossible, image to re-create in real life.

Consequently, many of us innocents watching began to believe that if only our parents were like Carol and Mike Brady, then all of our problems would be over. I found that when my parents didn't live up to these expectations, I felt betrayed. Later in life, I carried this to the next step, which was that every problem I had was in some way tied into the rotten way I was brought up.

Not nurtured enough, not approved of enough, not breast-fed enough . . . well, you get the picture. I've since learned that this blame game serves no one, especially me. Staying in the past was getting me nowhere, and I began to see that in order to fully live in the present and create the life I deserved, I would have to let my parents go.

This was by no means an easy task. My memory was long, and it wasn't pretty when I thought of my upbringing. I remembered with frightening clarity how my parents refused to give me baton lessons because it was too expensive. Who knew how many marching bands I might have sparkled and spun for if this hadn't been the case? Money, or the lack of it, was the deity in our house, so anything deemed too expensive—a dress for a dance or the latest fashion fad—fell by the wayside because, as my father told me no fewer than 100 times a day, "Money does not grow on trees."

Verbal and emotional abuse was part of my childhood, but what to do with this knowledge was the question. As I talked about in Chapter 1, I ate these feelings away with cookies and ice cream for years, trying to sweeten it all up, before finally realizing that the only thing that was growing was my waistline and not my sense of well-being. How exactly would I be able to let go when the two people who were supposed to love me unconditionally and give me all the peace and security I could ever want had let me down? The answer is that it happened gradually, one parent at a time.

My DAD WAS THE FIRST ONE that I changed my relationship with. He wasn't an easy person to get along with, and saying that is like saying that Attila the Hun needed space to grow. One Christmas, I was determined to give him a present he was sure to love, and I wasn't going to allow money to influence me. I thought and thought and finally decided to get him one of the portable boom boxes that were all the rage that year. He loved music, especially around Christmastime, and I envisioned the hours of carols he could enjoy with this great gift. I decided to buy him all of his favorite music on cassette tape, too, and imagined that he'd think of me when he was listening.

I believed in this dream, hook, line, and sinker, thinking I was going to turn his family room into Carnegie Hall. At that time, the players were the size of a small refrigerator truck, but that didn't deter me from buying one and gaily wrapping it in preparation for Christmas morning.

The day arrived, and I proudly presented my gift to him. I was convinced that this wouldn't fall flat like all my other failed attempts at making him happy with a gift. It simply wasn't possible. Dad opened the box with the expression of an excited child, but when he saw what it was, his face fell. He recovered quickly, but I knew he wasn't impressed.

A week or so later, I got a call from my mother. Quite timidly, she asked me if I had the receipt for my father's gift. She kindly explained that what my father had really wanted was a VCR.

I can't explain what happened next. It was like some demon took possession of my body, and I began to scream at my mother. Once unleashed, there was no taming my tongue. I told her that I was sick and tired of buying gifts that no one appreciated, and that furthermore, I'd flush the receipt down the toilet before I'd turn it over.

Then I did the unthinkable: I slammed down the phone and hung up on my mother.

I was breathing so hard and my emotions were so high that I felt as though I'd just boxed a round with Muhammad Ali. When I calmed down, I wrote my father a letter. I explained how hurt I was that he didn't appreciate this gift, or any of the presents I gave him throughout the years. It was cathartic because I found that as I wrote, I felt better. I wasn't mean-spirited; I just expressed my feelings.

It turned out that writing the letter was about a lot more than just the gift. It was about me standing in my power and not allowing how I was feeling to go unexpressed. Always being a good, never-rock-the-boat kind of girl, I often wouldn't express my anger or hurt feelings for the sake of keeping peace—but I'd done that long enough. I could no longer keep silent and had to take a stand.

I mailed the letter, and my parents and I didn't talk for a few days. Then my father called. He told me that he'd gotten my letter, and that after he read it, he posted it on the refrigerator right next to his all-important 50-cents-off coupons. This said everything to me, because I knew that he'd not only read what I'd written, but he actually understood what I had to say.

From that point on, our relationship changed. I became more accepting, and he became more considerate. He passed on five years ago, and it makes me feel so good to know that the last words we said to each other were: "I love you." I was able to let him go with no regrets, no hard feelings, and no words left unsaid. Not a day goes by that I don't think of him fondly.

That leads to the other half of this equation: my mother.

WHEN I WAS GROWING UP, she was like a ghost in many ways— Casper the friendly ghost, but a ghost nonetheless. When my dad passed, I realized more and more that although I'd had problems with him, the bigger issues were really with my mother. When my dad got nasty, where was she? This realization shocked me, because I'd always thought she sat just to the side of Mother Teresa. After all, she's a retired registered nurse and nothing gave her more pleasure than taking good care of us when we were sick. I mean, I was in

school before I realized that a rectal thermometer wasn't a natural part of my anatomy like a tail on a dog.

Once I started seeing her in this negative light, however, memories blossomed; and I realized that in many ways, my mother just wasn't there for me. I'd learned to be self-sufficient, which was a good thing, but it hurt me to look back and see all the times she'd told me to fight my own battles rather than stick up for me with the neighborhood bullies.

Why all this was coming up at my age was anybody's guess. I'd really thought that I was done with blaming my parents, but there it was, smacking me in the face. The question was: What was I going to do about it?

My dad's death had a curious effect on my mother. Instead of transforming into the freed butterfly that I expected, she became more and more needy. She wanted and expected my siblings and me to take up the slack my father's absence had created. I came to understand how much my father had done for her. The first time she told me that she didn't know what she was going to do about her toenails being clipped, I didn't get the connection until she told me that my dad had always done it for her. I answered promptly that I couldn't even remember the last time my husband touched my feet, let alone cut or acknowledged my toenails, so I didn't feel that it was a job I was going to undertake anytime soon.

Still, I felt a twinge of guilt. My tendency is to want to please the people I love, and my mantra to my mother soon became: "What can I do to make you happy?" It was a question that should have never been announced to her once, let alone become a sacred chant. After five years of trying to fulfill her unreasonable demands, I wanted to contact the church to see if I could nominate my dad for sainthood because of how he'd put up with my mother's "needs."

I REMEMBER ONE LATE-NOVEMBER DAY when I picked my mother up to go shopping. It doesn't take a witness stand for me to admit that I took her out of guilt. I knew that I had no time to be involved with her that day, but she called and just had to get out, so what could I do? I dropped her off, then left to attend to my own errands.

I was running around like a lunatic because it was two days before Thanksgiving, when I'd be entertaining 20 people for dinner. To make matters worse, I'd just lost my kitchen ceiling in a flood of water due to a Jacuzzi gone terribly wrong. When I finally finished with the tasks on my to-do list, I went back to pick up my mother at the appointed time and place, where we'd agreed that she'd be waiting. Alas, she wasn't where she'd promised to be.

I finally tracked her down inside the store, finding that she was sitting on a chair merrily chatting with a saleswoman as if she had all the time in the world. I felt my blood beginning to overheat. Yet I put a smile on my face and told her that I'd been waiting outside for 20 minutes. My expression was so tight and forced that it looked as though I'd just had a really bad face-lift.

"Mother, it's time to go," I repeated through gritted teeth.

She stood up nonchalantly, gazed at me, and said, "I hope you remembered my house key, because I do not have it."

Rage filled me. On the inside, I morphed into the Incredible Hulk mixed with Russell "phone throwing" Crowe on a bad day. I didn't have her key, and I knew this meant even more time to track down someone who did. I couldn't believe that she had the nerve to take up more of my day.

As we walked outside, I began to yell, which was a reaction I never expected to have, despite my anger.

"Get in the car!" I shrieked.

You have to picture this heinous scene. My mother is just over five feet tall and shrinking, so she looks like the typical kindly little old lady who might bake you a fresh apple pie. The other shoppers looked at me in astonishment: How dare I scream at this sweet senior? I'm sure some of them were considering calling the "Abuse to Granny" hotline, but I didn't care. It's not like anyone was ripping her dentures out.

I'd crossed over to the dark side, and there was no turning back. We got in the car, and there was dead silence between us. I finally got her key from the main office of her building, then rushed her in the front door and promptly left.

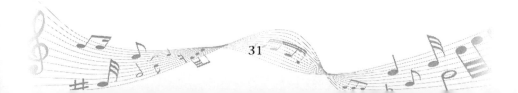

Immediately afterward, I began to question my actions. *What the heck had gotten into me?* I knew this outburst was wrong on every level. *What had driven me to behave in such a way?*

I realized that I was doing things over and over again out of guilt. I was being manipulated into feeling that I was the one person who held the key to her happiness. I wasn't coming from a place of loving-kindness at all. This had to stop, because at my mother's age, something horrible could happen to her after a stormy session like this, and I'd regret it for the rest of my life.

So I called her after a few hours and apologized. My mother told me off soundly, and I listened because I knew that I deserved it. Something in me had shifted, though. This wouldn't happen again.

AND IT DIDN'T HAPPEN AGAIN . . . until, of course, I decided to invite her to Florida, thinking that it would be just the ticket to make her happy. As I described earlier, I have two homes, splitting my time between Sanibel Island in Florida and Buffalo, New York. My family lives up north, and when I'm in Florida, my husband commutes between the island and Buffalo. Even though it was my time to live in Florida, I'd decided that I'd fly back up in order to escort my mother.

We got on the plane, and I was bubbly with happiness. We were going to my home on a lovely island, which truly is a paradise in every sense of the word. Once on board, my mother looked at me in a panic and told me that she was cold. What would she ever do if she caught a chill!

This is something I've heard my entire life, but I've never been quite clear about what it means—especially coming from a registered nurse. Even a rectal thermometer doesn't know what she means. All I *do* know is that if you catch this dreaded thing, you're in deep trouble with dire consequences. One chill and your head could fall off!

My mom began to bundle up, and the next time I glanced over, she looked exactly like the Unabomber with her hood pulled up and tightened to the max. She even had on her extra-strength sunglasses to ward off any eye chills. All I could think was that at any moment a sky marshal was going to approach and arrest us for being some kind of terrorists. She could have ended up being dubbed Osama Bin Mama.

Finally, we landed in sunny Florida, but Mom was still in chill mode—and I don't mean that she was relaxed. All she could discuss on the drive to my lovely island home was the fact that she was in dire medical straits. She was certain that she'd caught a dreaded chill on the plane, even though we were basking in 80-degree sunshine.

"I hope there's a doctor on this island of yours," Mom said in that way that always made my heart sink.

Why had I taken her on this trip? We weren't even there yet, and she was being so difficult. What had I gotten myself into?

The next day, all seemed fine, and her chill obsession subsided for the time being. That afternoon, I told her that I was going to work out and provided her with the number of the nearby gym in case of an emergency. Some 15 minutes later, I was stepping away on the StairMaster when the gym manager handed me the phone.

"Your mother," he mouthed, and I could feel my eyes begin to roll.

Barely able to breathe, let alone talk, I gasped into the receiver, "What is it . . . what is it?" Maybe she'd fallen? Or perhaps she was burning down the island. Surely, something horrible must have happened.

Well, it was horrible . . . for me.

"When are you coming home?" she demanded. "I'm getting lonely."

Gritting my teeth, I told her that I'd be finished soon. After handing back the phone, I attacked the machine so intensely that I almost stepped myself right through the floor.

The next morning, my mother told me that she needed help getting dressed. Only too happy to oblige, I agreed to provide some assistance. She handed me a pair of surgical stockings that looked pretty small to me. I realized that trying to get them on her feet would be like trying to fit a watermelon into a thimble.

I strained and pushed until it felt as though I was back at the gym or giving birth. After I got them on her, I asked who helped with these when she was at home.

She smiled and replied, "Oh, I do it myself. But it's nice to have you take care of it since you're here."

At that moment, I didn't know how I was going to survive the week. To say that she made it interesting is an understatement. By time the vacation was over, I'd taken her to the doctor because, yes, she was convinced that the dreaded chill had turned into *something* after all—even though the doctor could find nothing wrong. We also made more trips off the island in 48 hours than I ever had before due to the fact that she shopped, bought, had buyer's remorse, shopped, bought, had buyer's remorse, and on and on.

After the trip was over and we were back in Buffalo, I went to see my sister. She took one look at me and knew that my idyllic paradise vacation with my mother had gone terribly wrong.

"Mom is just impossible," I told her.

We both just shook our heads.

THE LAST STRAW IN THIS QUEST to make my mother happy actually happened only a few months ago. Ever since my father passed away, my mother had been looking for the perfect home. She was under the impression that new living quarters would solve all her problems and give her the happiness she was looking for.

Her first move was out of the house she and my father shared to a lovely retirement village. It was an idyllic location, and she had a patio home all to herself. We all thought this was the perfect place for her. After a few years, it didn't turn out to be the paradise she'd envisioned. So as her discontentment grew, my mother decided to move once again.

One aspect of my mom's personality that my siblings and I discovered only recently is that when she makes up her mind to do something, it has to happen yesterday. Luckily, my husband had recently found a lovely senior-citizen apartment for his father, and we were able to get my mother an apartment in the same building.

She went to visit and loved it, insisting that if she could have her way, she'd move in that very day.

My sister and I, along with our families, did all the work preparing for this move. Of course, my mother didn't so much as put a can of beans in a box. Instead, she was like a general directing her troops, and we jumped to her orders. It was a daunting job, but we finally got her settled into her new home, even though there were still things we had to dispose of in the old house.

A few days after the move, I took her out to lunch and sensed something wasn't quite right. I was exhausted and my intuition told me not to ask this question but before I could stop myself, I said, "Mom, is something wrong?" (Never ever, ever, ever say those words to an aging parent. I can tell you the answer is *Yes!* every single time.)

She began with a tirade about why she shouldn't have moved: This was a terrible place with terrible people. She was so unhappy. How could I have allowed this to happen to her?

I just looked at her and burst into tears.

My mother was shocked.

I sobbed and sobbed and couldn't seem to control myself.

"How can you be complaining already, when this move isn't even complete?" I cried.

She just sat there, stunned. For once, she was speechless, so I continued to cry (our waitress was kind enough to bring me a box of tissues), and as I released those anguished tears, I felt something shift.

Something released. I truly could not do this anymore. I realized that after five years of serious work and guilt, I couldn't make my mother happy—nor was it up to me to do so.

From that moment on, I gave myself permission to do things for her when I wanted to rather than because I had to. My resentment began to subside, and I was able to find a more compassionate outlook. My dad—her best friend—had died, and my mom was lost. She was demanding and trying to fill this void, but it was an impossible task. I also understood that the times in my childhood when I felt that she'd let me down had to be released. That was an absolutely freeing feeling.

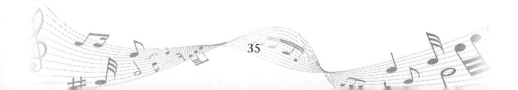

Now I take her "issues" with a sense of humor. The other day, Mom told me that she was going to run away with the maintenance man whom she was sure had a crush on her. I told her a kindly good-bye, saying that I wasn't sure if he'd clip her toenails. I could laugh at the situation. I've learned to let go.

MY ADVICE IS TO REALIZE THAT, above all else, our parents are human. Trying to get by day after day in the best way they know how is a tough job at age 70, 80, or 90 and worried about the future. As grown children, we can find all the ways they failed us and allow those missteps to haunt us for the rest of our lives. Or we can attempt to make them happy, when in truth, it's impossible. The best option is to release them—to let them follow their own paths and be who they are—and in so doing release ourselves as well.

Just don't catch a chill, or you're doomed.

❖ ❖ ❖

CHAPTER 5

Don't Stop Till You Get Enough

When it comes to presents, I'm the one who never stops giving. In fact, I believe that Kool & the Gang wrote "Celebration" after watching me figure out how to honor, celebrate, and yes, party down with the special people in my life.

I've sent flowers, planned events, and bought more gifts than I care to count. This doesn't come easily because I put a great deal of time into my choices, driving myself crazy trying to select the perfect something for someone or plan the perfect party. I'll impulsively send flowers for no specific reason, and I get a great deal of pleasure from the surprise I know this generates.

I love giving, and heaven knows I have it down to an art. However, it's also fun to receive once in a while, and this is where there seemed to be some misunderstanding.

Don't get me wrong. It's not as if every time I do something, I expect the same in return. It's just that when I receive a gift, I like to imagine that more thought went into it than planning a fast-food lunch.

I'LL NEVER FORGET ONE CHRISTMAS when I'd shopped until I dropped. I planned and found the perfect tribute for everyone on my list. Yes, Santa was working overtime, and she was exhausted. The burden of holiday shopping has always fallen on my shoulders because my husband feels that since he works and earns the money, it's somehow beneath him to help in the selection and purchasing process. No elf work for him. Thus, the only person my beloved has to shop for is me. He has the burden of one.

With wide-eyed anticipation, I awoke on Christmas morning. Everyone opened their gifts with "Oohs" and "Ahhs" of delight. Then it was my turn, and I couldn't wait to see what my husband had carefully chosen for the love of his life. In fact, I even took my time opening my big gift, the special something from my honey. After carefully removing the bright red wrapping, I attacked the box. The first thing I saw inside it was something that resembled roadkill.

Certainly, this couldn't be! I refocused my eyes and realized that the dead hunk of fluff was a collar of some kind—fur! He'd actually gotten me some kind of fur coat! I couldn't believe it. How many times had I told him that I was against them? I'm a woman who would brake for a bird crossing the road. I didn't want to wear someone else's hide on my back. Realizing that I needed to actually hold the garment, I took the jacket out of the box to get a really good look.

Maybe I was being too harsh at first glance, and it was fake. But no, this definitely had belonged to some kind of animal—species unknown—and it was attached to a tiny, formfitting, leather bomber jacket. It looked like it might have fit me when I was six years old and lacking hips.

My husband smiled and walked further into the fire by telling me proudly that it was indeed real fur. I tried to smile and gently asked him where he purchased this jacket. He then enthusiastically told me where he always purchased his gifts.

I cringed because the place was notorious for only giving credit, no refunds, and all thoughts of going to one of my favorite stores to replace the coat with something a bit more appropriate vanished as quickly as my daughters when the dishwasher had to be emptied. I couldn't stop myself from bursting into tears.

My daughters were aghast at my reaction, and I must admit that I was a bit shocked myself. After all, Christmas is all about giving, right? It was just that after the thought I put into everyone else's gifts, I couldn't believe that he'd bought me a present that was totally *not* me. Unless I was going to lose about 100 pounds, join a motorcycle gang, and run off to parts unknown, I couldn't use this jacket.

I knew what had happened. My husband had run through the store ten minutes prior to closing on Christmas Eve and grabbed something with an exorbitant price tag, probably off the mannequin. That would account for the pint size of this thing. If he were married to Twiggy or Calista Flockhart, and they were hunters in their spare time, then this would have been the perfect gift. But he wasn't married to them. He was with me, and a fur ball that didn't fit was his version of a thoughtful gift.

The fact that I wouldn't be able to return it and get something I might really want made the entire situation too difficult to bear, because it meant that I actually had no gift. I couldn't hide my disappointment and set a far-from-wonderful example of Christmas gratitude for my family. But I didn't care, because my feelings were demolished.

I must admit, though, that I did consider whether there could be a case of heredity at work. I remembered my father and the boom box I'd bought for him. Was there something in my genes that just didn't allow me to appreciate what I was given? I thought about this seriously, but then I decided the situations were definitely different. I'd put a great deal of time and effort into my father's gift, and that was not the case with my husband's shopping.

This was a turning point for me. I decided that I was no longer leaving things to chance. If I really wanted something, I might as well buy it for myself. The chances were good that even with all the hints I dropped and pictures I left out, I wouldn't get what I really wanted from anyone else.

From that point, Christmas chores took on a new flavor. I still shopped for my loved ones, but each time I went to the stores on that sort of mission, I picked something out for myself, too. Oh, it was just a bangle bracelet here or a new journal there. It didn't need to be anything expensive—just something showing me that I appreciated all I did. And if it was something I really needed, I was covered, which was easier than dropping all the unheeded hints.

I couldn't believe how well this little trick worked. I loved the seasonal shopping and no longer felt like a world-class martyr doing it. On Christmas morning when I was faced with a bunch of gifts that were the wrong size, the wrong item, or the wrong color, I could cheerfully show appreciation because I knew that everything I really wanted was in my closet already. I learned to give to myself.

At first, this notion may seem very selfish, but I came to realize that if I couldn't give freely to myself, then I wasn't really being generous with others. I was so caught up in what I was giving away, and had such huge expectations about what I should get in return, that I set myself up for disappointment. In all fairness to my family, it was very difficult for them to fulfill my ideals. By learning to buy myself presents, I discovered how to show myself gratitude and appreciation.

Since I didn't have such high expectations of my family anymore, I appreciated their gestures more when they actually showed up. Their presents took on a new meaning as I embraced this concept. I could even chuckle at my husband, knowing he just wasn't a shopper and was doing the best he could. I didn't need my loved ones to give me what, in truth, I could only give myself.

THESE DAYS, I SEND MYSELF beautiful flowers, too. That's right, I send *myself* flowers. I started doing this when I was in the midst of planning a surprise party for my mother-in-law. While I was busily completing all the preparations, I kept thinking how nice it would be to get flowers just telling me "Thank you" for doing such a nice job with the event. I'd had this fantasy before, and it had never been fulfilled. Then I thought, *Why couldn't I just send myself flowers?*

At first, the idea seemed bizarre, but I started to dial the florist before I could change my mind. I told the woman on the phone exactly what type of flowers I wanted: I love stargazer lilies and having their sweet fragrance in my home. As I described my perfect bouquet, she could tell from the conversation that the flowers were for me.

She said, "Of course, there will be no card."

I quickly said, "No, I would like a card."

In a voice of utter disbelief, she asked me what I wanted it to say. I didn't hesitate to reply, "Thank you, Susan, for all you do. Love, Susan." My answer came with confidence and sincerity.

The voice on the other end of the line chuckled good-naturedly and told me that they'd be delivered the next day.

When I woke up the next morning, my first clue that it was going to be a day to be reckoned with was the sound of pouring rain. *Naturally.* I was planning a pool party, but it seemed that could only be considered good if you were a duck or a fish. I got up and decided to forge ahead, thinking maybe the weather would clear up. No chance. And from there, things slid even further downhill.

I went out to pick up a few last-minute things, and I lost my car keys in the store. I had the entire place looking for them with me, and I could tell by their pitying glances that they thought I was one banana short of a bunch.

I couldn't believe it was happening, since I would have to do the unthinkable. I would have to call my husband—who must tell me at least 1,000 times a day how unorganized I am—that yes indeed, I'd lost my car keys. He listened sympathetically, but that wasn't fooling me. I knew what was going on in that macho mind of his, but I knew I wasn't going to give him a chance to say anything.

He came by the store, took one look at my face, and wisely decided this was not the time for one of his world-famous wisecracks. Handing me the extra set of keys, he ran to his car like someone being chased by a rabid raccoon. That wasn't far from the truth.

Right after I finally got home, the doorbell was ringing. I frantically looked at the clock, thinking it couldn't possibly be the guests arriving already. I opened the door, and standing there was the flower deliveryman.

I paused, soaked it all in, and felt so good looking at those beautiful flowers. I breathed in the heady scent of the stargazer lilies, and I loved the brilliant pink and white blooms that completed the arrangement. *Just perfect,* I thought. Everything fell into place as I put them in a vase and opened the card. I read, "Thank you, Susan, for all you do! Love, Susan."

What a feeling that gave me. I smiled for the first time that day. I knew someone was grateful for all my hard work and cared enough to say thanks. It was all I needed.

I put the card up in a prominent place, and every time during the party when someone asked me who sent the flowers, I showed them the card. They all laughed, but then admitted that they thought it was a great idea.

After the party, I moved the card to my kitchen; and throughout the week, it prompted me to thank myself often and well. Since then, I've called the florist and arranged deliveries on random days with cards saying things such as "Have a nice day." I always sign them, "Love, Susan."

This really works to brighten up any kind of day. And if you're thinking that it's much too expensive a practice, keep in mind that you can buy in any price range; the key is simply having them delivered. It just gives that extra spark and is another way for you to remind yourself that you're something special.

I'VE ALSO LEARNED TO GIVE MYSELF the pleasure of my own company. In the past, I often couldn't go to the movies I wanted to see because they were "chick flicks" that my husband just wasn't interested in. Now, I go by myself if no one wants to accompany me, and the bonus is that I don't even have to share my popcorn. I've gone out to lunch, to museums, and to art galleries alone, realizing that I really am good company.

I'm a huge Black Eyed Peas fan, and they were in concert in Las Vegas when my husband and I were scheduled to be there. I asked him if he'd like to go and he grimaced at the question.

"You want me to sit and listen to rap?!" was his incredulous response.

My heart told me that he'd much rather be sitting at the blackjack table, but I really wanted to go to that show. I knew that if he was unhappy, I would be, too, but I could never go to a concert alone—or could I? As I started checking out the tickets, I wasn't getting very good seats when looking for two together. Just for the heck of it, I decided to see what would happen if I looked for one seat. The selection was incredible, and I found the perfect spot right near the stage.

"I can get a great seat if I go to this concert alone," I said.

"You'd go alone?" he asked, as if I'd just suggested that I would dance through the streets naked. His question was like waving a red flag in front of a bull.

"Sure . . . why not?" I said, and quickly bought the ticket before I could change my mind.

The day of the concert arrived, and no one could believe I was going alone. My daughters told me that the older I was getting, the nuttier I was becoming; but they all agreed that they admired me as well. Mom going to a rock concert alone was actually pretty cool.

When I walked to my seat, I was amazed. I was actually sitting in the VIP section. I'm not a namedropper, but let me tell you that Eva Longoria and her then husband Tony Parker were sitting behind me with Mario Lopez. Just as I thought I couldn't be any more excited, I looked at the row in front of me and—could it be? Yes, it was! There was Fergie's husband in the flesh—the incredibly hot Josh Duhamel. Although he now stars in movies such as *Transformers*, to me he'll always be my beloved Leo from *All My Children*. I was snapping so many pictures of all the stars around me with my phone that I was getting a cramp in my thumb. My family couldn't believe the company their mother—who was "all alone"—was keeping.

The music started, and I danced my socks off. I knew that if my husband had been sitting there, I would have been anxious about whether or not he was enjoying himself. Was the music too loud? Was I dancing just a bit too crazy? But because I was alone, I didn't have to worry about any of that. All I had to do was have a great time and enjoy myself—and I did. It was one of the best concerts I've seen in my life, and I think a big part of it was due to the fact that I was alone and pleasing only myself. To think that I might have missed this experience—truly a once-in-a-lifetime event—cured me of thinking that the only way I could enjoy something like this was by going with someone else.

I do like the company of others, but it's a wonderful thing when you can truly enjoy your own company. Giving to yourself can be a foreign concept. As a woman, you might be programmed to give to everyone else at the expense of yourself, losing a part of who you are in the process. It doesn't require a big budget to splurge on yourself; it just takes the courage to admit that you deserve it. After that, everything becomes easy, and you'll find more ways than you can imagine to show yourself just how extraordinary you are.

❖ ❖ ❖

CHAPTER 6

Let's Get Physicals

Once a year, it rolls around. The date is circled on my calendar. My heart skips a beat as it looms closer . . . and closer. Is it my birthday? I wish. Instead, this is the date (or a few of them) when I get all my physical tests done. It reminds me of high school, because once again, these are exams I truly want to pass.

Ah, medical tests. I feel at times like a prisoner during the Inquisition being tortured to come up with the right answers. I know it may sound as though I'm overstating it a bit, but that's how I feel. Unlike my mother, who views doctor's visits as high points on her social calendar, I dread them with a passion. *Iatrophobia* is the clinical term for this fear of doctors, and although I don't have a full-blown case, I'm mighty close. As I'm getting older, this particular anxiety is getting worse. I blame my mother, because when it comes to health issues, she always came up with horror stories that would make Stephen King proud.

WHEN I WAS IN MY 20S, GOING to the doctor meant I was either sick with a minor illness or pregnant. These are mostly innocuous visits. This all changed the time I went for my annual physical, and I found out my blood pressure was high. My doctor said it with the warm manner I'd become accustomed to over the years. He's neither a "McDreamy" nor a "McSteamy," like the doctors from the show *Grey's Anatomy*. He's a thin man who wears bow ties. He looks like the kind who would still make house calls, although of course he doesn't, because he'd probably be kicked out of the AMA. Still, when he says something, I listen.

At first, I was surprised that he was telling me I had high blood pressure, but then I thought about the fact that I got anxious just walking into his office, so I explained this. He dismissed my anxiety theory as the complete culprit. My mind scrambled and I thought, *Maybe I'm just a little high in this department.*

"This is nothing to fool around with," he solemnly told me. "There's no such thing as blood pressure being a little high. It's like saying you're a little pregnant."

I was beginning to get alarmed.

"I want you to go out and buy a blood-pressure machine and monitor your blood pressure four to five times a day so that we can get an accurate idea of where it is," he said.

He gave me a prescription for medication and told me to call him after I'd done my own readings for the next few days. I couldn't believe that at this stage of my life, I was already following in my mother's footsteps. Of course, I was being told time and again that I was now at "that age"—whatever the heck that meant.

But I was very aware of the blood-pressure station my mother had at her house, along with notebooks filled with graphs and charts of hourly blood-pressure fluctuations. Could this truly be in my future?

I felt doomed as I ran right to the pharmacy to fill the prescription and get my own blood-pressure machine. I took it home and started reading the directions as I prepared to take my first reading. Once again, I felt myself getting anxious just adjusting the cuff. It follows that my first numbers were high, and I began to panic.

What if I have a stroke right here and now? I thought. *I'd better start the medication.*

I took my medicine, waited a prudent amount of time, then took my blood pressure again. Still high.

Oh my God! I thought, scrambling to take it again . . . and again. Each time, the readings kept climbing higher and higher. In fact, my arm was getting bruised from the cuff since I was using it so many times.

In desperation, I called the pharmacist asking if the medication I was on had any unusual side effects, like making my blood pressure higher rather than lower. He said with astonishment in his voice that he'd never heard of anything like that and highly doubted it. I explained what was going on with my home machine, and he suggested that I come into the store because he knew their machine was accurate. I never thought that perhaps it was just a technical snafu! Obviously, it was a problem with the equipment.

I ran out the door and got to the store in record time. Sitting down at their machine, breathing as though I'd run a marathon, I took my pressure. It was higher than at home.

At this point, any reasonable person would understand what was going on. I was obviously too stressed out to get a normal reading, but logic had jumped ship and left behind Suzy Stressed. I was in a full-tilt adrenaline rush reminiscent of the carbon monoxide scare during my college days

I went home feeling that at any moment I was going to drop dead. I called the doctor's office with my results.

"Oh, that's not good," he said with concern. "We'd better increase the medication and continue to monitor your blood pressure."

I groaned and agreed. When my husband came home, I was at the dining room table with the blood-pressure cuff on and meditation music blasting in the background.

"What's going on?" he shouted. "And what is that beeping noise?"

"I am taking my blood pressure!" I screamed. "And I need peace and quiet!"

He shook his head and ran up the stairs. He knows that when I get caught up in one of these health-concern obsessions, it's best to leave me alone.

During the next few days, the beeping of the machine became a steady sound in our home. The pharmacists knew me by name and were considering charging me rent for the amount of time I was sitting at their blood-pressure machine. At one point, I actually hip checked an elderly lady to get to the machine before she did. I was that desperate.

My results varied but never fell to the normal range. The more obsessive I became, the worse the readings got. After a week, I'd had enough. My arm was almost permanently tattooed from the blood-pressure cuff, and my entire life revolved around the next reading. Sanity began to return, and I realized that as long as I was this hyper, I'd never get a normal number. The constant beeping of the machine was giving me a migraine, a problem I didn't want to have to deal with since it would mean more tests and more meds.

So I threw the machine in the garbage and stayed away from the pharmacy, which by then I couldn't even pass without my pulse racing. I continued with the medication my doctor had prescribed and figured I'd wait for my next appointment to see where I was.

When the day came, I was a nervous wreck, thinking what my pressure might be. I was on my medication faithfully, but who knew? The doctor and I began chatting while he examined me, and the physical was just about over. Could it be? Had he actually forgotten to take my blood pressure?

I was beginning to feel like Tom Cruise in the latest *Mission: Impossible* movie. I'd averted the crisis and could skip out on the torture. I totally relaxed and got ready to leave, so I glanced around for my purse. At that point, before I knew what was happening, he took my pressure . . . and lo and behold, it was perfectly normal.

He smiled his best Dr. Non-McDreamy smile, and out the door I went, vastly relieved. Amazing that relaxation was the cure for what ailed me!

NOW THAT I'M "THAT AGE," I find my doctor's visits are full of perils. It's interesting that no one ever really defines what "that age" means. Does it change depending on the phases of the moon? What exactly does it signify? My analysis is that you're at a point where you're beginning to fall apart piece by piece. Your doctors will begin to give you more tests to prove that fact, and then try to patch you up like a used car. So because I'm "that age," once a year, I enter the front lines of my annual physicals like a soldier going into battle.

My first stop recently was at the gynecologist, and the exam began with the dreaded weigh-in. The nurse has been there a long time and always goes along with my story that I just weighed myself, so she doesn't need to do so because I can tell her my actual weight with great accuracy. I do this every time, promising myself that by the next year, I'll actually be at the number I'm telling her. I just know that one of these days it will catch up with me. That crisis averted for one more year, I entered the room where the real fun begins.

I saw the table, the stirrups, and all the test strips ready for action. My doctor came in, and we sat down for the chat.

"Have a seat and put your feet in the stirrups, please," she said.

There's a smiley face on the ceiling so that I could stare at it while I get poked and prodded in the orifice that a gynecologist is interested in. The image was a kind thought, but it didn't really divert my attention too much from the discomfort. After all, there's only so much a smiley face can do

"We should do a rectal exam," she began, "because . . ."

"I know." I finished for her: "because I'm at 'that age.'"

"Everything seems fine," she said, "But it's time for your mammogram and we should do a bone-density test, too."

Oh fun, I thought. Nothing quite goes with a rectal exam like some bone-density peril.

I got home and figured that I'd better call to make the appointments for the tests. I knew that if I waited, procrastination would set in and I wouldn't get them done. Because the bone-density thing was new for me, I thought I'd also better ask a few questions, including: "I'm not going to have to go into any kind of tube for this test, am I?"

EVER SINCE I GOT STUCK IN AN ELEVATOR with 30 freaked-out travel agents, closed spaces have been a bit of a challenge for me. This elevator incident happened in Hawaii in a luxury hotel that I was visiting with a group of travel-agent colleagues in order to assess the amenities. I knew as we all crammed in and the buzzer went off that there were too many of us in too small a space.

The doors closed, and the elevator descended about two feet before it stopped dead. At first, there was total silence as we all digested the fact that we weren't moving. Then the woman leading the group, the one who was supposed to be in control of anything that could possibly go wrong, began to panic, screaming that she couldn't breathe. Others began to get unsettled as well, and we attempted to contact someone to assist us, using the phone in the elevator.

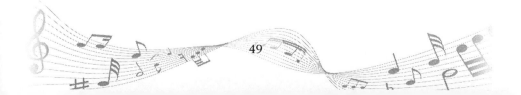

The person we reached did nothing to inspire confidence, and we all decided to use whatever tools we had in our purses to pry the doors open. We managed it with combs, keys, and nail files. Never underestimate a group of motivated women! We found that we were just a few feet below the floor, so we all climbed out, and the manager of the hotel quickly escorted us to the bar for an unending supply of complimentary drinks. The last thing he wanted was for this story to make the travel-agent rounds. Since then, I take the stairs whenever possible.

HEARING THE TREMOR IN MY VOICE as I asked about the nature of the bone-density test, the woman on the phone quickly assured me there would be no going into tubes or other small spaces. I breathed a sigh of relief as I got off the phone. That appointment was set, so it was on to my general practitioner.

This doctor reminded me of all the other tests I needed. My blood work was due, my skin needed to be checked, and my thyroid should be scanned.

Does it get any better than this? I wondered.

Getting it all taken care of was starting to resemble a full-time job. I called the mammogram lady back to see if I could have all the fun and excitement on the same day, and she quickly set it up for me. I could swear she recognized my voice.

The last test to schedule was with the lab for my blood work. I knew that this was going to require fasting, so as much as I wanted it all done on the same day, I knew that there was no way I was going for a mammogram on an empty stomach. What if I fainted while my breast was pinned in the machine, fell to the floor, and ripped it off? I could actually visualize this happening, so I figured that I'd better head to the lab the day before.

THE DAY OF MY LAB WORK arrived, and I'd dutifully starved myself the night before. Why is it that I never get hungry at night except when I know that I can't eat? As soon as my dinner was finished, I started stressing over the fact I couldn't have another bite. I wore a path to the refrigerator just to open it and stare longingly at all the things that I couldn't touch. I went to bed early with my stomach growling.

The next morning, I arrived at the lab bright and early with at least two pounds off my behind. The blood work went smoothly; I looked away from the lab tech, who was taking vial after vial of my blood.

"Boy, your doctor takes a lot of tests," she smirked.

I wasn't amused, and panic began to set in as I imagined all the exotic diseases she was checking me for in each one of those tubes.

"Okay, we're all set," the tech said.

I felt as though I'd just been drained by one of Sookie's vampire cohorts on *True Blood*. Then she handed me a cup.

"What's this for?" I asked.

"We need a urine sample," she said.

What? I wasn't prepared for this, and although I'd downed my water in the morning, I'd also gone to the bathroom right before I entered the lab room. Normally, I have to pee every five minutes, especially when I'm traveling on a cross-country flight, sitting in the window seat next to a self-important businessman who rolls his eyes every time I have to get up to use the bathroom. In that moment, however, I didn't feel so confident.

Armed with the little cup, I marched off to the bathroom, found the toilet, and waited for the flow. Nothing! I turned on the faucet, hoping to stimulate a response. Although I felt like I was sitting next to Niagara Falls, my bladder didn't cooperate. I couldn't believe it.

After sitting for what seemed like hours, I finally felt an urge and pushed and panted as if I were giving birth. I quickly placed the cup under me to capture this liquid gold, but I could feel it going everywhere except in the cup.

Where is it coming from exactly? I thought as I shifted the cup around and around. *I need a bigger cup!* I wanted to shout.

The pee had stopped, and I was almost afraid to look in the cup. I pulled it out and furtively glanced at the contents. There were approximately 20 drops of urine collected in this blasted thing. Dejectedly, I washed my hands—which I'm sure collected most of this specimen—and sheepishly handed it to the lab tech.

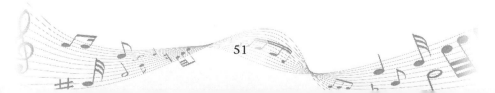

"Is this going to be enough?" I asked as I caught her exchanging glances of pity with one of her colleagues.

"Should be," she said with some skepticism.

Overjoyed to be finished, I ran out of the lab before she changed her mind.

THE NEXT DAY I HEADED FOR MY MAMMOGRAM and the other assaults on my body. It was beautifully sunny outside with perfect white clouds floating across the sky. A glorious summer day, and I was avoiding thinking about what horrific things might have invaded my body. Luckily, I was armed with good-health affirmations I'd learned from Louise Hay's book *You Can Heal Your Life*.

I am grateful for my healthy body, I said to myself and smiled as I approached the receptionist. She handed me some forms, and I completed them. She also gave me a pager.

"Do you know how to use this?" she asked.

"I've used them at restaurants." I answered. "Does this mean that when the pager goes off I can expect a good table with a great breakfast and a Bloody Mary, please?"

She laughed and then said they were trying to turn this whole thing into a spa experience.

"Well, a bar may be a good place to start, with mimosas on tap," I said.

"We're starting with your bone density, then mammogram, and last your thyroid scan, okay?" she explained.

What kind of spa treatments are these? I thought. I would much rather have had a facial, hot-stone massage, and pedicure.

Please don't think that alcohol is the only thing on my mind, but at that point I could really have used a stiff drink. Instead, I sat and flipped through a magazine until the pager buzzed. Needless to say, there were no plates of eggs Benedict or Bloody Marys waiting.

I was off to the bone-density test, and as promised there was no tube to go into—but there was a scale. I'd just begun following one of the best weight-loss plans I'd ever tried, and it was really working. At that point in my life, I wasn't yo-yoing anymore, and this plan was something I could finally live with. The one issue was that I couldn't weigh myself for 21 days, and I was only on day 3.

In a timid voice, I told the woman that she could weigh me, but I was facing away from the scale and didn't want to know the number. She totally understood, and I was proud of myself for telling her exactly what I wanted.

The test was uneventful, and the woman told me that I'd have my results in a few days. It was one of those things where no news is good news—meaning the doctor would only call if there was a problem.

Next step, mammogram: I stripped to the waist and again waited for my name to be called. As the time passed, I felt myself getting more and more anxious until finally a cheery technician called my name. I walked with her into the room and faced *the machine*. A sadistic group of men had to have invented it. I can see them sitting around, thinking about how best to see the inside of a woman's breast. After much discussion, one finally said, "I know, we can get two plates, place the breast between them, and flatten it to resemble a thin-crust pizza. That should do the trick." And so it was decided. Was there payback in there for some of the injustices that men perceive women as having done to them?

My breasts aren't petite. The technician took one look at me and said to her colleague, "We're going to need the bigger plates."

They set up the machine, and for some reason this technician was having a great deal of trouble getting my breast positioned just right. After ten minutes of wrestling with it as if she were going a round with Hulk Hogan, I gently asked her how long she'd been doing this job.

"Oh, for years and years." she answered.

Frankly, I didn't believe her. I began to think she might have been in cahoots with the men who invented the machine.

She finally got a good picture of the first one, and we moved to the second one. Again there were problems, and at one point she had my breast pinned in the machine with me in a position I'd seen a Cirque du Soleil performer achieve the last time I was in Vegas. I

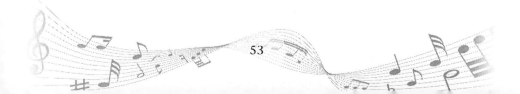

was so uncomfortable that I was using deep-breathing techniques and visualizing lovely beach scenes so that I wouldn't pass out.

Finally, we were finished. I was so glad to get out of that room, I truly wondered if I'd died and been caught in some kind of mammogram hell. One positive thing about this facility was that they gave the mammogram results immediately, so off I went to wait for the results, still wondering if I needed a bag to breathe in so that I didn't hyperventilate.

My name got called once again, and the doctor told me I had "happy breasts" and that all was well.

"Thank God," I said sincerely, sending out a prayer to all the women who may not have been so fortunate.

There was only one more test—the thyroid scan—which is primarily someone running a jelly-filled tool over my throat. It was cold, but something I could handle. The exam went smoothly, and I also had to wait for these results.

I'm not really someone you'd call patient, so I wished I could get all the information on the spot, but at least the tests were finished and I could go home and relax. On the way out, I said good-bye to the receptionist and thought, *This is one spa I'm happy to be leaving.*

A week went by, and I got a call from my gynecologist's office. I wasn't home, and the cryptic message just said, "Please call back during business hours." I loved that because of course I received the message at 6 P.M. on a Friday, which meant I had to wait until Monday to learn whatever this call was about.

It has to be about my bone density, I thought, hoping that they were calling to say everything was fine, even though I knew that wasn't the protocol. Those results come in the mail. I was trying to stay positive, since believe me, I know I overreact to all this stuff.

Monday arrived, and I placed the call. The first attempt failed as the nurse-practitioner, who was apparently in charge of this news, was in a meeting. She finally called back and told me that the doctor wanted me to have more blood work done.

"Did they test for calcium and vitamin D in your annual lab work?" she asked me.

"I don't know," I answered. "But I do know they took enough blood from me to keep the Cullen family from *Twilight* happy for a week."

She wasn't amused. "The doctor needs to see you immediately," she said. "And if you don't have those results, we'll need more blood work done."

I was getting concerned and decided to do the unthinkable and ask her exactly what this was all about. She curtly responded that I had osteopenia.

"Is that some kind of Italian dish?" I asked.

"This is no laughing matter" she responded. "If this isn't addressed, it could turn into osteoporosis."

Finally, something I could understand. I breathed a sigh of relief that this wasn't some type of rare disorder and thanked her.

On my journey through life, one thing I've wondered is why doctors and their assistants don't tell us what's going on in language we can understand and with some sort of compassion. I don't want to say that it never happens, but most of the time they're strictly business, and I'm too intimidated to ask questions. I'm happy to say that's changing for me, though, and once I knew exactly what I was dealing with I felt much better.

THIS WAS ALL HAPPENING TWO YEARS after my first blood-pressure fiasco, and I must admit that after all the anxiety I'd had, going to my new general practitioner seemed almost anticlimactic. I knew this doctor well. She'd replaced my old bow-tie-wearing doctor and was someone I could actually relate to. I knew if there was something really horrible in my results, I would have heard from her already, so that gave me some confidence. I'd meditated, done yoga, and listened to soothing inspirational music on the way to her office. Even though I was worried that I might actually fall asleep at the wheel, I was doing everything in my power in to be sure my blood pressure wasn't elevated.

I sat in the waiting room . . . and waited. This is one thing in life that's truly appropriately named. They may put TVs in those rooms, along with hundreds of magazines, but the bottom line is

that you're waiting. Finally my name was called, and I resumed meditative breathing in order to keep my blood pressure in check. I felt that old anxiety yearning to pay a call, but I'd learned that relaxation was key, and I had the tools necessary to make it happen.

The nurse-practitioner weighed me, and once again I said that I didn't want to know my weight. We chatted a bit, and I was in the zone. Before I knew it, she'd taken my blood pressure, and it was normal—first hurdle overcome. I waited a bit more for the doctor to arrive.

I like my doctor, and we'd probably be friends if I didn't feel that she held the fate of my life in her hands. She studied my results and began to explain all the numbers to me. Overall they were okay, but not great.

She looked at me solemnly and said, "You know what you have to do, don't you?"

I sighed and nodded. This was the dance we did every year. I knew—and she knew that I knew—that I'd be a medical miracle if only I got rid of the extra weight. As I said earlier, I've accepted my plump Mae West figure. But I also know that as I get older, this excess weight is impacting my health.

The 21-day plan I'd begun just before this battery of tests was working, and I vowed to get it done. I told the doctor all about it, and she wholeheartedly agreed that it was the plan for me. But the last thing she did actually blind-sided me a bit.

"It's time for you to get a colonoscopy. You are that age," she said.

I went home and told my husband that everything was fine, plus the part about the extra exam. He shared that he'd been getting the same message from his doctor about the colonoscopy, and I got a brilliant idea.

"Let's get this test done together," I suggested.

He looked at me dubiously. Many of our friends have had this procedure, and I knew the prep for it was primarily drinking a wicked concoction that kept you on the toilet most of the day. Who wants to be going through that when your partner is enjoying pizza and wings?

"We can prepare together the day before. It will be fun! Like a colonoscopy date!" I said, knowing that I was pushing it on the fun part, but reluctantly he agreed.

I called to schedule our appointments, and the woman informed me that we'd need a ride home from the hospital where we were getting the test.

"No problem," I told her, and my mind started racing. Who would take us and pick us up? I decided to ask my oldest daughter.

"You want me to do what while you are doing what?" she asked. She knew how her father was about anyone driving him anywhere, and she didn't see this happening.

"Dad will be fine with it," I merrily told her.

"Okay . . . I guess," she replied.

I got off the phone before she could change her mind.

The day before our date with our colons arrived, I had all the stuff on hand to clean us out. I set up everything, and my husband just looked at it and groaned. Still, we downed our first drink together, and he retired to the basement to watch TV. Sometimes I truly believe that if he stays out of the basement for too long a time, he'll get altitude sickness.

The drink had barely gotten to my stomach, and I immediately had to go to the bathroom. I ran, and sure enough, things were percolating at rapid speed.

My husband heard the toilet flush and yelled up the stairs, "You can't possibly be on the john already. It's only been five minutes since we drank that stuff. *Seinfeld* isn't even over."

I'm blessed with wonderful regularity, and my husband not so much, so my bowel habits were always a source of amazement to him.

"You'll go soon, too," I told him, as if this was just the most wonderful event in the universe. I went to the bathroom about 50 times in the next few hours, and my poor husband didn't go once. As we moved on to our second dose, he finally began his cleansing. We were getting ready.

The next morning, my daughter arrived to pick us up, and I was still sitting on the john.

"Where's Mom?" she asked, and my husband sourly responded that I'd been in the bathroom 23 out of the last 24 hours. For some reason, all this wasn't really bothering me. I was looking at it as a good detox that was only lasting one day. Maybe I'd even shed a pound or two on the colon cleanse diet!

My husband drove us to the hospital, and we checked in. Of course, my mother had already shared a few of her colonoscopy stories with me, including the procedures gone terribly wrong; and I was trying to keep these ideas out of my head.

"Aunt Mary had one of those tests, and the doctor perforated her bowel. Had to go in a bag for the rest of her life. I hope your doctor has steady hands," she told me. Thanks, Mom.

As we got prepped, I did glance at the doctor's hands, and thankfully they weren't shaking. We got the tranquilizer drip going, and the nurse asked us who'd like to go first.

"Me," I shouted. I didn't want to wait.

"Would you like to watch the procedure?" she asked. "That way we won't use as much sedative."

"Sure," I said, feeling it was safer for me to keep an eye on the doctor and be able to stop him if I noticed any trembling of the hands. Waving a fond good-bye to my husband, I left feeling really relaxed.

With one deep breath, the procedure began. It was pretty amazing to watch what was happening on a small TV screen. As the doctor moved through my colon, I found it interesting and thrilling that he wasn't finding anything to be concerned about. We chatted through it all, and before I knew it, I was laughing as the nurse wheeled me back to the room.

My husband looked at me in the most incredulous way. "How can you be talking and laughing? Didn't they knock you out?"

"I didn't want to be knocked out. I wanted to see what was going on."

He took one look at the nurse and said, "I don't want to talk or see anything. Give me enough of that stuff to stop a hippo."

This is the same man who, when asked if he wanted the mirror in the delivery room moved in order to watch the birth of our daughters, kindly declined. He didn't want to see a thing and felt the same way about his own colon. Off he went.

Thankfully, he, too, passed with flying colors; although when he put the doctor on the spot and asked him who had the better colon, the doctor smiled and pointed to me.

"That young lady has a very clean colon," he declared.

That's one of the nicest things anyone has ever said to me, and I smiled at my husband in a superior way. My daughter drove us home with my husband grumbling about her driving skills, and I know she was thrilled to finally drop us off.

I didn't even run to the john.

Another year's tests were over and done. All in all, my results were fine; and deep in my heart, I knew that good health is the ultimate blessing. I'm just grateful that my tests supported that fact. I also know that the chances are better that I'll drop dead of a heart attack waiting for doctors, their calls, and their test results than ever getting diagnosed with any exotic disease.

Remember: breathe . . . just breathe.

❖ ❖ ❖

We Are Family . . . on Vacation

For as long as I can remember, I've had a fantasy of the perfect family vacation. My dream travel plans are full of breathtaking scenery and a family doing everything together with smiles on their faces the entire time, having so much fun they can't stand it.

As a child, the only family vacation I remember that didn't involve visiting relatives was one year when we went from our western New York home to Frontier Town in the Adirondack Mountains. I think I was about nine or ten at the time, and my brother and I were beside ourselves with excitement.

When we arrived, it turned out that Frontier Town was basically a bunch of condemned buildings with over-the-hill cowboys and horses that looked as though they were one step from permanent retirement. It seemed this was the place the old cowboys went to before they died, and they'd brought their horses with them for good measure.

This Old West re-creation was just plain *old* in every sense of the word. As the gunfights played out and the broncos were busted, it seemed that everything moved in extra slow motion. Even at such a young age, I began to fear for the safety of all involved . . . especially the gunslingers. One could drop over at any moment from old age.

Even worse was the fact that this trip just didn't live up to any of my expectations and certainly paled in comparison with my friends who had gone to the Mecca of family vacations: Disney World. When I was a child, we didn't commune with Walt and Mickey because, in my father's words, "It's just too damn expensive."

After the Frontier Town debacle, he informed us that the next year he was buying a swimming pool, and all our family vacations from then throughout eternity would be in our own backyard. Basically, I'm saying that I felt family-vacation deprived. I vowed things would be different when I had my own brood.

THE FIRST TIME I COULD BRING my plan to fruition was when my three daughters ranged in age from seven months to five years. The company my husband worked for at the time owned a 30-foot motor home, which was available for management to use. My husband booked the RV for two weeks in April, and we were actually going to Disney World. Not only was I making my dream come true, but I was also creating the vacation of a lifetime for my daughters.

We lovingly packed the motor home with the mountains of essentials that might have looked excessive . . . to a man. At one point, my husband commented that it would be easier to have just gotten movers and brought our entire home with us. His words flew by me because I was high on all the excitement, and nothing he could say was going to put a damper on this trip.

As the sun rose over Buffalo on the appointed day, we pulled out of our driveway with the girls in their frenzied state of anticipation. None of us had slept one wink.

"They'll sleep on the road," I assured my husband. He just rolled his eyes as we began our trip of more than 1,000 miles at 6 A.M. The girls were golden. In fact, we were on the road about two full quiet hours . . . and then the whining began.

My five-year-old had the nerve to ask, "Are we there yet?" Maybe it was the excitement of crossing state lines.

Yes, only two hours into our road trip, and we'd already read books, played games, and exhausted all the amusements that I thought would keep them occupied for two long travel days.

"I thought you said they were going to sleep," my husband repeated. Was this going to be his only vacation conversation?

"Let's have lunch," I proposed. "No need to pull over as I can prepare everything while you drive."

This was in the days before anyone was really concerned about seat belts, and the girls and I were walking around the motor home without a care. Of course, I opened the refrigerator just as my husband encountered a bit of bumpy highway. The noise was deafening as the soda cans crashed to the floor and burst open. The girls started shrieking, and my husband was yelling expletives I only hoped the kids wouldn't repeat at the next family gathering or in a school paper entitled "Family Togetherness."

"You can't open that fridge when we're going this fast," my husband yelled.

Why is it that men are so good at stating the obvious after the fact?

"How am I supposed to know that?" I screamed back. We gave each other looks that said we'd both better shut up while I cleaned up the soda mess in silence.

After the girls were happily fed, it was time to breast-feed the baby. I let out a sigh of comfort as I eased into the captain's chair next to my husband and began to open my top. My eyes were closed, and I was just beginning to relax when my husband let out a howl that rivaled James Brown on the radio.

"What are you doing now? Don't you know we're at eye level for the trucks that are passing, and every single one of those drivers can look in and see you? Where are your brains? They'll get on their radios and tell every driver within miles that a woman is exposing herself in an RV camper," he ranted.

I began to get a picture of a brigade of trucks following us all the way to Florida, just to get a glimpse of my daughter having lunch. I felt he'd totally lost his mind because the truth was that you could see absolutely nothing but the back of a baby's head and my naked neck, which had been on display in two states already. It wasn't as if I was like Janet Jackson having a wardrobe malfunction in the Super Bowl halftime show.

Knowing this wasn't worth the argument, though, I moved to the back of the RV and all hopes of serenity vanished as the other girls vied for my attention. My dreams of family bliss on this vacation began to fade.

Still, we got to Disney World one day early as my husband was making land-speed records to reach the Magic Kingdom. We didn't arrive soon enough. The walls of the RV were beginning to close in, and I was truly afraid of what we might do if we heard "Are we there yet?" one more time. This included feeding one of the girls to Minnie Mouse.

But we were finally within Walt's clutches, and I was filled with excitement when we entered Fort Wilderness, the special campground on Disney World property. We approached the front desk to check in, and our smiles were wide. Road trip? What road trip? The girls were absolutely ready to swim, hike, and mix with superstars such as Camper Goofy and Fort Wilderness Mickey Mouse.

But there was a problem. We *had* arrived one day early, after all.

The girl behind the desk looked at us as though we'd just arrived from Mars and incredulously told us that there was no campsite for us. Didn't we realize it was spring break, which was their busiest time of the year?

"We might have a cancellation, so you can try a bit later, but I highly doubt it. That almost never happens," she chirped, opening her magazine and dismissing us with a wave of her hand.

Dejected, we walked out much as the Griswolds did in *National Lampoon's Vacation,* when they were told that Walley World wasn't open. I thought my husband was literally going to cry. Like the chipper Julie on *The Love Boat,* I told my family not to be discouraged as there were tons of campgrounds around, and we were sure to find something even better for one night. I knew none of them believed me, but I stuck to my story as we got back in the camper and proceeded to be told "No room at the inn" at about 100 campgrounds.

My husband's driving skills were really being tested, too, because it wasn't easy to maneuver a 30-foot camper in and out of some of the places we were sent to. At one point, after almost rear-ending an 85-year-old lady who was going about 25 miles an hour, he pulled over and got out of the vehicle. Dad was beyond overboard.

I believe that's the closest he ever came to totally deserting us. I could swear I heard him say that he wondered if it was possible to get some kind of asylum in Cuba. Luckily, he didn't get a small boat. Instead, he got back in the RV, and we drove back to Disney while I prayed for that cancellation.

My prayers weren't answered. The same girl now had a disgusted look on her face as she basically told us to scram.

It was late. Everyone was cranky and tired. As we pulled out of Fort Wilderness, my husband noticed a huge parking lot meant for people going to the amusement park during normal hours. Without any discussion, he pulled in, and with a no-nonsense look on his face said, "We are parking here."

"How can we park here?" I asked. "There are signs everywhere saying no overnight parking."

"It's late. No one will check. We will be fine," he said with a look that told me he didn't care about any signs.

What choice did I have except to resign myself to the fact that our first night in Disney World was going to be spent in an Orlando jail? Maybe Goofy would frisk me. I could just see the headlines in the newspaper the next day with a picture of all of us behind bars: "Family of Five Arrested for Overnight Parking in Disney World." And on top of all of this, an orange jumpsuit wasn't a fashion statement I was looking to make any time soon.

Yet we parked, because it was well past midnight and the girls were fast asleep. Hunkering down next to my husband, I couldn't help but notice that he was snoring blissfully while all I could do was stare at the ceiling.

Just as I was beginning to doze, there was a pounding on the door.

"You in there—you can't park here. Open the door!"

The Disney police were on to us. I had a vision of a strictly dressed police officer, wearing Mickey Mouse ears.

"Don't answer the door," my husband hissed. "They'll go away."

They did go away, but they returned every hour on the hour. The only bright side to this was that the girls were so exhausted they didn't even stir. Finally, security returned one last time and threatened to have the RV towed, so my husband sleepily hoisted himself out of bed and started the engine. Yes, we left the parking lot.

Luckily, it was morning, so we were able to get to McDonald's where Egg McMuffins had been our gourmet breakfast for the past three days.

Finally, check-in time arrived, and we were able to pull into our campsite. The older girls promptly ran away to explore, and in our first hour there, I had to contact a park ranger to help me find them.

The only thing that had been lost for good was my oldest daughter's tooth, which was the reason she'd disappeared. She'd dropped it and was under the misguided notion that she could find a baby tooth in Fort Wilderness. She'd wandered farther and farther away from the campsite with her sister in tow. When they were located, I was so relieved that I couldn't even yell at them. Much better, I promptly put them to bed, although it was only 5 P.M. We needed some rest at that point, and I think even they knew better than to complain.

The next morning, armed with our passes, we were optimistic and filled with the magic of Disney. We walked into the park, and—there were lines, miles of lines at each attraction in the Magic Kingdom. This was in the dark ages before Disney thought up the Fastpass. We had to line up . . . forever. I pulled the family to Country Bear Jamboree and gleefully told them that regardless of how it looked, the line would move quickly.

Sadly, this wasn't the pilot of a new show called *Mother Knows Best.* That line had so many zigs and zags that it could have been a ride all on its own. When we finally got in to see those damn Country Bears, the two older girls fell asleep, and I had to find a way to feed the baby without causing an international incident. (Was this another reason I might be put behind bars—"Mother Breast-feeding Infant in Country Bear Jamboree"?)

After that, the girls whined through It's A Small World—and I'm going to say here and now that it took me a few months to get that tune out of my head. They were then terrified by the Pirates of the Caribbean and threw up on the Dumbo ride.

By the time it was over, and we were leaving for the two-day drive home, I couldn't be held accountable for what I might do at any mention of Mickey Mouse and his magical home. I also decided that an RV of any size wasn't big enough for our family. Maybe the next summer I'd break ground for that swimming pool.

BUT JUST LIKE THE INTENSE, MIND-NUMBING moments of labor, I soon forgot about the negatives. So each year we ventured out, only to have the trips fall short of my unrealistic expectations.

All of this came to a climax after I decided that it would be fun to become a travel agent. The girls were getting older, and this was an occupation I could sink my teeth into. I went to travel school, graduated with flying colors, and began to work part-time in a busy travel agency.

Armed with my new credentials, I knew that I'd plan the annual family vacation and, unlike all the failed attempts of the past, this one would be perfect. I was an expert, after all.

I'd always wanted to take a cruise, and with the benefit of a travel agent's discount, there was no reason why I couldn't do so. Gingerly, I presented this idea to my husband, and he did his usual eye-rolling thing, but didn't say, "Hell, no! I won't go!" Any married person knows that this means "Yes."

My daughters were all for it because as a family, we'd never done anything quite so glamorous. I was thrilled and on a mission to make this the most excellent vacation of our lives. Of course, even with my discount, I was still on a budget. So, I examined the rates and what was included, and I decided there was no reason why the five of us couldn't share a cabin. The sleeping arrangements were set up for five, and after all, how much time would we really be spending in the room? There was so much to do and see.

I made all the plans, and we anxiously waited for the day of departure, which began with a flight out of Buffalo and touchdown in San Juan, Puerto Rico. We were right on schedule—this was a great sign. Yay! A bus transported us to the ship, and we checked in with no issues. We were given our on-board credit cards, which were just like cash, the cruise director explained to us. I looked at each of my daughters and told them sternly to guard their cards with their lives. My husband just snickered, and off we went to find our cabin.

I'd splurged a bit for an outside cabin, so I was already imagining myself sitting comfortably, sipping my morning tea in a chair gazing out the window at the sea. When we opened the door, we all looked in and then collectively jumped back in utter and total shock.

"Is this the closet?" my husband asked.

As I looked around and realized this was our home for one week, I thought, *I can't let them see me sweat. I'm a professional.* So I plastered a smile on my face and said, "This will be fine. We just have to stay organized."

My daughters looked dubious and were already prepared to jump ship with their cruise credit cards.

"Where are we going to put our luggage?" my oldest asked. She was the one who had a makeup case that held enough cosmetics to create new looks for an entire tropical island filled with not-so-glam natives.

Like the optimistic Mary Poppins, I began to point out all the places the luggage could be stored, including under their pillows.

"Why don't you put some of the bags under the beds?" I trilled.

"Those are the beds?" my husband skeptically asked. "I thought they were couches. Actually, they look more like love seats."

"Oh come on," I said and found that I was beginning to hyperventilate as the reality of this situation took hold. We really were going to be together in this walk-in closet for one week, and it looked as though once our luggage was in the cabin, there would be no room for us. My husband went to sit on the bed/couch and was playing with the television remote when he came to the stark revelation that he was only going to have access to two channels. I decided the best thing to do was to escape and head for the bar.

"Dad is the best organizer in the world," I shouted as I ran out the door.

I thought, *Ahh, a nice soothing drink will make this all better. Something with an umbrella in it will take the pain away.* Food was the last thing on my mind, despite the fact that my last meal was the day before. Armed with my on-board credit card, I ordered the biggest tropical drink on the menu. It was something that came in a pineapple and had about 100 shots in it. As I sipped and sipped some more, I immediately began to feel better.

We'll make this work, I told myself. *They just need to look at the beautiful ocean we'll be sailing on.* Just then the ship's horn blew, signaling that we were departing. With one final slurp of the straw, I emptied that pineapple of every bit of alcohol it possessed. As I got up, I felt a little tipsy but hightailed it to our cabin because I felt this was a family moment we couldn't miss. Please—I watched *The Love Boat* enough in the '80s that I had to wave at the shore surrounded by my family.

Back in the Cabin From Hell, everyone seemed to be doing okay, and my husband had indeed gotten things put away. Another plus: no one had killed each other yet. We all headed to the deck. As we watched the shore disappear, we truly shared a feeling of well-being. I'm sure my drink enhanced my Zen moment, but it was my little secret. We had the early dinner seating, so, after departure, we all headed down to the dining room.

"Make sure you all have your credit cards, so you can do what you like after dinner," my husband announced, and when I opened my purse to check for mine, I realized that—*oh my God*—it was gone. In a flash, I had a clear visual of it sitting on the bar next to my pineapple. I quickly told my family that I had to check on something and ran to the bar. The bartender looked at me with genuine sympathy as he told me that no one had turned in my card. I couldn't tell my husband about this faux pas. After the lecture I'd given my daughters about responsibility, how could I tell them that before we'd left the port, I'd already lost my card?

For a brief moment, I closed my eyes and saw a college student here on spring break who was now using my card to buy the entire ship drinks at about $10 a pop. I ran to the office, but no one had turned the card in there, either. The women I spoke with recognized that I was at the point of a hysterical breakdown and quickly reassured me that no one had used my card. She canceled it and issued me a new one. The first crisis was successfully diverted—but the seas were about to get even rougher.

My oldest daughter found out that she was old enough to drink legally on the cruise ship, so she came home night after night a bit tipsy and then stepped on my husband's head as she climbed up to

her top bunk. A riot also broke out in our cabin when three menstruating woman attempted to share a bathroom barely big enough for a hamster. At a dinner when the ship was rocking and rolling, we all left the table one by one to throw up, except my husband and the preteen boy of the family sharing our dinner table, who thought that the spareribs were pretty good and ordered double desserts.

Suffice it to say, this cruise was bedlam. My husband never left the ship at any port. When I asked him why, he said it was the only time he had any kind of peace . . . *when we left.* One of the two channels on the TV was playing *The Ten Commandments* movie in Spanish every day, and my husband had become a bilingual Charlton Heston fan by the end of the cruise.

I learned lessons that not even my on-board credit card could buy during my time on the open water. I found out that no matter what the brochure says, five people can't fit into one cabin unless it's the size of an apartment. I also learned that a family of five in close quarters like that can behave much like the contestants on the show *Survivor.* And no, you can't eat your young.

We now refer to that trip as the family root canal.

AFTER THE CRUISE HIT THE SKIDS, I didn't throw in the towel on family vacations, but I did lower my expectations. I knew that the trips of my dreams weren't possible because they were based on an idea that was totally unrealistic—a fantasy befitting a science-fiction movie. A family on vacation was just that—a family with all the warts and thorns it displayed at home, except with everything heightened because we were putting it on the road and being forced together pretty much 24/7. I had to realize that just being together was enough.

Now that everyone's older, we talk about all the vacations I considered failures at the time. We have stories to share that literally have us laughing so hard that we're crying. They were never perfect, but boy were they a lot of fun in hindsight. The family has grown, and husbands and grandchildren have entered the picture. I continue to feel the pull of bringing everyone together for a big group vacation, and each time I do there are tears, drama, and arguments galore.

But when it's all said and done, the one thing I know above all else is that we're family, and coming together once a year is worth every minute of imperfection. We're creating memories, the stuff family is truly made of that will be shared and bring joy for a lifetime.

And that swimming pool . . . I did buy it after all. If anyone wants to breast-feed a child on the deck, it's fine with me.

❈ ❈ ❈

CHAPTER 8

Forever Young

Even though I've made great strides with my anxiety and medical encounters, I still hyperventilate just making an appointment with the dentist. Why? Because I'm sure that when I go there will be pain and a diagnosis of something dreadfully wrong with my mouth—for instance, that I'll loose all my teeth within six months and have to live forever on soup and Jell-O.

My dentist is very progressive and tries to create an experience that isn't like dental death row. In fact, he has a bevy of dental hygienists, each one jollier than the next. I'm sure they've been told that most people are terrified just walking into the office and their job is to make the experience as pleasing as a Caribbean cruise (and no, not the one I described in the last chapter).

This particular day, my hygienist greeted me at the door and introduced herself as if we were at a cocktail party. However, she didn't fool me for a minute. I didn't see any bottles of wine chilling or hear any martinis being shaken. She chatted merrily and had a sunny disposition that was almost a bit too cheery, if you know what I mean. Looking at my chart, she told me in the tone of a nursery school teacher scolding a preschooler that not only had I missed my six-month checkup, but I hadn't been there for more than a year. She did all this with the broadest smile on her face.

"Have you been having dental work done elsewhere?" she asked.

Shocked, I responded that I in no way had been unfaithful to my dentist and had not cheated on him at all. The truth was that time had gotten away from me, and I couldn't believe that it had been over a year. She smiled at me indulgently, and I actually felt relieved to be back in her good graces.

As I was escorted back to the examining room, I noticed the soothing pictures lining the walls and the upbeat music playing in the background. They were doing their best to make me feel relaxed, but all I could think of was the great latte I was going to treat myself to when this was over. Nothing better for a sparkling set of clean teeth than the stains of a nicely brewed cup of coffee. Why not live a little?

All I had to do was get through the next hour. To begin, I got into a state-of-the-art chair, and although it was designed for total comfort, my body was barely touching it. I think I was actually levitating.

Relax, this is just a checkup, not a root canal, I silently reminded myself.

I began to calm down just as the hygienist told me that it was time for x-rays. *No big deal,* I thought, until I had to bite down on a little piece of plastic that tore into the bottom of my mouth—about 20 times.

"Ohh, I know that's tender," Miss Sunshine said. "Just a few more and we'll be done."

At this point, I truly felt that she'd x-rayed each of my teeth individually, but finally we were done. It was time for the next step, where she did some kind of measurement on my gums and shouted out numbers. I knew from the past that I didn't want a number above three because that meant I was in danger of gingivitis. In all honesty, I didn't know exactly what that was, but I did know it involved more trips to the dentist. Any disease with such dire consequences was one I wanted to avoid at all costs.

While I was diverting my gaze to avoid staring directly into Miss Sunshine's eyes, I noticed a chart that said, "Get rid of the 11s."

Oh my God, I thought. *What are the 11s? Is that some dreaded new periodontal disease? If a number greater than 3 was bad, what could an 11 mean?* I had a vision of a mouth like a Halloween jack-o'-lantern with teeth that were black and rotten. Was this something worse than the dreaded gingivitis?

As I quickly scanned to the bottom of the chart, I noticed the word *Botox* in large bold print. I was so startled that although the hygienist had her entire hand in my mouth and was an inch away from touching my tonsils, I had to speak.

"Is someone here doing Botox?" I mumbled.

"Oh yes," she replied, as though this was the greatest news in the world. "The doctor is."

With giddy excitement, she proceeded to give me a sales pitch on the glories of Botox. Of course, the "11s" this chart referred to were frown lines. But with one quick trip to the dentist, all the worries could be magically erased from my face—even the frown lines that were forming a month earlier from thinking about making a dental appointment!

As she continued to list all the advantages of Botox injections, I had to interrupt once I could feel my tongue again and tell her that she had no idea who she was talking to—or should I say "pitching."

I'm leery of vitamins because of possible side effects. I read the warning labels on every medication I take and in no way would ever consider letting someone shoot my forehead full of something that had part of the word "toxin" in its name. Hadn't I heard that this toxin was something that had killed the pioneers? I truly felt this was an answer to a question I'd recently heard on *Jeopardy!* Wouldn't there someday be a medical report stating that one of the side effects from Botox injections was your head falling off? No thank you.

I thanked her kindly for the information, and she continued her work.

As she was cleaning my teeth with a high-powered water tool that sounded and felt as though it could blast every tooth out of its socket, my mind began to wander. What is the world coming to with this perpetual search for the fountain of youth? When did we elect the housewives of Beverly Hills as role models for aging gracefully? I'm sure that what they spend on cosmetics and plastic surgery would be enough to get the United States budget out of its deficit.

Recently, my daughter told me that she'd been invited to a Botox party. It was similar to a Tupperware party in theory, but instead of getting stackable airtight containers, she could get an injection that would ensure her face was airtight. She and her friends are only 35. What is this obsession?

At my dentist's office, I could now get my teeth cleaned *and* wrinkles removed. Throw in a good teeth bleaching, too. I could leave with no lines on my face and a grin white enough to illuminate an entire darkened room. I could tell my husband that we

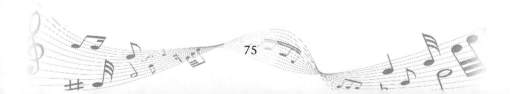

wouldn't need a generator to power our house if the lights should go out. I could just smile.

As I lay there in the chair, I thought about how we're bombarded with this idea that the idyllic woman stays forever young. If we aren't going to opt for surgery, we can buy $100 jars of cream that will keep our face that of a 20-year-old's. Recently, I went for a facial. It was my first, since I'm more of a massage kind of girl, and I didn't know what to expect.

While we were walking to the treatment room, the woman asked me what my facial regime was. Facial regime? Was washing at night considered a regime? I embellished a little, but pretty much told her that I washed my face with a facial cleanser and applied some moisturizing cream. I didn't dare tell her that I'd only recently graduated from Dove soap to a facial cleanser.

We went through about a 40-step process to restore my face to the youthful smoothness of a baby's bottom. After it was over, she told me about all the products she used and how they were all naturally organically based.

All I could think of was how we Baby Boomers are using all the blueberries and green tea on the planet. Of course, it would make the most sense to purchase the products so that I could develop the real *regime* of facial care she solicitously explained. When I glanced at the price of the cream that removed the circles from under my eyes, I saw that it was $300. I'd look like a raccoon before I spent that kind of money. I told my facial therapist that I didn't have my purse with me and would return to buy all 40 of the products when I'd put a second mortgage on my home. She chuckled, but I was serious—so much for my regime.

I recently saw Betty White at 89 years old, receiving a Screen Actors Guild award, and while I don't know for sure, she doesn't look to me as though she's had any "work" done. Her face appears natural for her age, with lines I'm sure she earned and wears proudly. She looks like a spunky grandmother who has aged well. Old chronologically, yes, but young in the sense that she hasn't lost her zest for life and is living it to the fullest.

I think so many people are so caught up in battling the years that they forget to enjoy them. Let's face it: Have you ever seen a good face-lift? Not long ago, one of the women that I meet every once in a while at the gym had her back to me as we were talking about the weather. When she turned around, I gasped. Her face was pulled so tight that she had a perpetual smile, similar to the Joker in *Batman*.

"Wow." That was all I could say.

"Don't I look great?" she asked. Then she dropped the bomb: "I'd be happy to give you my doctor's number. He is a miracle worker."

Was I insulted? No. Would I call him? No way. I'd rather see him turn water into wine than work on my face. I just smiled and nodded in response. I couldn't understand what she saw when she looked in the mirror. Sure, her wrinkles were gone, but I thought she'd lost all the character in her that those lines represented. She didn't seem real anymore.

Come to think of it, I don't recall anyone I know who's had plastic surgery and does look better. And the movie stars I've seen? Suffice it to say that there's no proof there. If these people who have money for the best end up looking like they're wearing some kind of Mardi Gras mask, what hope is there for us mere mortals?

I may sound like I'm being too judgmental about this, and I do understand that there can be a real need for this type of surgery. If a little nip here and a little tuck there makes a woman feel better about herself, I'm all for it. What I don't understand is the compulsion to change over and over again in an attempt to create something that just doesn't exist. In those cases, I think it's all about a woman's definition of perfection, holding herself up to an image that's impossible to achieve, and, most important, what she sees when she looks at herself in the mirror.

THE GOOD NEWS ABOUT ALL THIS CONTEMPLATION was that my appointment was just about over. My dentist came in for the final check, gave my mouth a clean bill of health, and off I went to get my well-deserved latte. I realized that I'd learned something besides the fact that I had to floss my back teeth better.

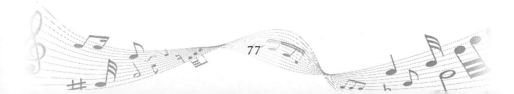

I discovered that I believe aging gracefully is an art not defined by face wrinkles and a chronological number. I'm embracing this part of my life with the creaky joints and, yes, those 11s on my face.

I'll wear my years proudly. I refuse to be defined by a society that focuses on looking young at all costs. I have no intention of making an appointment with a plastic surgeon to have my face frozen, lips plumped, or anything lifted up or sucked out. My wrinkles are my badge of courage. They represent where I've been and I am taking them with me in this next part of my life.

What's the diagnosis? My breasts sag, my fanny has fallen, my tummy goes out instead of in, and my cellulite . . . well, let's just say that I'd have to buy the cream by the barrel to tighten it up. Yet all of these well-earned life-road marks are part of who I am. With the physical aging comes emotional, mental, and spiritual aging as well; and I like how far I've come in those respects. I've learned more and more each year, and I'm proud that I'm always up for trying something new.

On my last birthday, I actually bought myself a bright pink Vespa. Contrary to my husband's ominous predictions, I haven't killed myself on it by wrapping my bod around one of the island's palm trees. I use it whenever I'm living in Florida. I enjoy the freedom, and although I wear a helmet that practically covers my entire body when I hit the gas, I enjoy the feeling of flying. I'm certainly not worried about wind damage to my face.

I'm soon going to be taking lessons to learn to paddleboard. My family members have all assured me that there's no way they can envision me peacefully paddling around the island's calm waters, but I'm determined; and when I'm determined, I can accomplish anything.

I'm grateful that I've been blessed to be on this planet at this time in history and have witnessed all that I have. I invite you to look at your life and all that you have to be proud of and grateful for. Remember that on the day you were born, you brought your unique and special light to this world and, as Mark Twain is reported to have said, "Age is an issue of mind over matter. If you don't mind, it doesn't matter."

⊞ ⊞ ⊞

CHAPTER 9

We Have Only Just Begun . . . Again

My husband and I have been married for 42 years, which seems like a very long time, even to me. Factor in the fact that I met him when I was 15, and without a vast amount of math, it's not hard to figure out that I've been with one man for the majority of my life.

We've grown together in many ways, and in others, I still feel as though I'm dealing with that 17-year-old boy who first captured my heart more than four decades ago. The one thing I can tell you for sure about this marriage is that *nothing is for sure*. It's as ever changing and fluid as a river winding down a canyon. In order to navigate the twists and turns, we've learned to have a sturdy boat and some really big paddles.

Let's start at the beginning: I met my husband at an amusement park. I'd seen him before our official meeting and knew he was one of the popular boys. Ah, he had an athletic build with long, messy brown hair and dusky brown eyes. Looking back at all this, an amusement park was the perfect place to begin, because our relationship has had all the thrills of a roller coaster, the collisions of the bumper cars, the dizzying repetition of a merry-go-round, and the romance of a tunnel of love. As a matter of fact, we shared our first kiss in the tunnel of love, where he was horrified when I "slipped him the tongue," as he puts it, which was my first experiment with the exotic French kiss I'd heard so much about.

He was a good Catholic schoolboy, and I was one of those "fast chicks" from public school. The times were much simpler, and a French kiss could actually be shocking. From that point on, it was determined that I was the adventurer in the relationship. After all, I was the one who brought France into it, and that wouldn't be the first time I'd expand our horizons.

That day began our 40-plus-year journey together. We were married when I was in my last year of college, and we set up housekeeping in a small upper flat. I was content and began to assume the role of the domesticated female of the '70s. It was a tumultuous time, though, with the Vietnam War, the civil rights movement, and feminists burning their bras. As my university was progressive, I was more of a flower child than a domestic goddess, but I tried my best to figure out exactly what this whole wife thing meant.

I must admit I did enjoy the lovemaking, and it was truly lovemaking for us. Believe it or not, even with the advent of the birth control pill, I walked down the aisle as a virgin. Although there had been plenty of petting (do they still call it that?), we'd never gone all the way. I was convinced that no matter what pill I took, somehow, someway, those little sperm cells would meet my eggs, and I'd get pregnant. My father, who held me to an 11 P.M. curfew until the day I said "I do," wasn't someone you'd ever want to go home to and tell that you were in the family way. So lovemaking was new to us as a couple, and it was sweet, romantic, and exciting. I've never regretted that I waited or that he's the only man I've ever made love to in this lifetime.

The other parts of being a wife were new to me as well. I had to learn cooking and housekeeping while marching for peace in Vietnam and justice for African Americans. No one called it juggling or multitasking in those days. My plate was simply full, and I enjoyed the wifely arts and learned relatively quickly. My mother-in-law was a cook extraordinaire, so those were big shoes to fill, and I didn't even try. I just puttered around making simple meals, and everyone lived.

There was a problem, though, and thus began the first adjustment I had to make in our marriage. My husband had no sense of time and was always late. We've joked that at his funeral, we're going to wait until 15 minutes after the service begins to roll in his casket, so he can literally be late for his own funeral—just like Elizabeth Taylor requested. When we were dating, it was a minor issue, and I assumed that he was still on his best behavior. Once we were married, he figured that he didn't have to try to be on time, and believe me, he didn't.

I'll never forget the first home-cooked meal I made. I was so proud of my roasted chicken, creamy mashed potatoes, and sugar sweet peas with onions. I mixed a chef salad with my own homemade dressing and waited for him to get home from work. He'd assured me that he'd be walking in the door at 5:30 P.M., promptly after work. The table was set and it looked like something that would be recognized years later as a Rachael Ray moment.

Well, 5:45 rolled around and no husband. Then it was 6 o'clock—no husband.

Finally, at 6:45 P.M., he strolled in the door acting as though he didn't have a care in the world, while I was furious. My chicken was shriveled and looked like one of the women in Miami who stays out in the sun way too long. The mashed potatoes were cold and runny, and the salad was so wilted from swimming in that dressing that it was more like soup. He could tell by my steely look that things weren't good.

And then, if there had been any doubt left, I started screaming at him. In those days, I was a screamer; and once I began, it didn't matter who could hear me. I yelled so loudly that had there been sound ordinances, I would have broken them.

"Where were you? Dinner is ruined! You said you'd be home more than an hour ago," I bellowed.

Out came the magic words I've heard so many times in our marriage that if I had a dollar for each one, I'd be richer than Bill Gates and Warren Buffett combined.

"I got tied up," he said.

What does that mean? In the early years, I took this at face value and actually got a visual of a crazed group of renegade outlaws lassoing him and tying him to a tree. Later on, I realized this was a catchall phrase that could mean anything from having to work late to stopping and helping out a friend by sharing a beer with him at the local bar. I remember that night as our first fight, and that flaw in his character was something we fought about often.

A great deal changed over the years, though, and this issue required one of the big adjustments on our journey. First, being late was in his nature. He actually believed that he could do things

in 30 minutes that took an average person 60 minutes. We argued over this, but nothing changed. He just lived in a parallel universe where his time was different from everyone else's, and if he wasn't punctual, then we all should understand because that was just the way it was—or the way *he* was. He wasn't selective about his tardiness. Be it family, business associates, or flights to catch, he didn't discriminate. He was simply always late.

This came to a climax for me when our second daughter made her First Communion. We'd been married 11 years, and all I can say is that I guess I'm a slow learner. She was all dressed up and needed to get to the church before us, so I drove her, while my husband assured me that he'd be ready when I got back. We had two other daughters, and both were dressed and ready to go, along with the First Communion girl and me. All he had to do was get himself set.

I dropped her off, rushed home and discovered to my horror that he was just getting out of the shower.

"We have plenty of time," he told me.

"We're going to be late. Parents are already starting to arrive, and the priest isn't going to wait for you to start the ceremony," I responded.

I saw no other choice but to pile the girls in the car and wait. Finally, he strolled out of the house 15 minutes late. Although this doesn't sound like much, I knew that the First Communion march was going to start right on time. Sure enough, we arrived to see my poor little girl sitting in the pew all by herself, trying to hold back the tears. The rest of the church was full; and as we walked down the aisle, I swear every person there turned around and looked at us—or maybe *glared* would be a better word. I even felt looks of disgust coming from the priest and altar boys.

Right then, I had one of those enlightening moments: *Why did I wait for him?* I had my own car. Why didn't I just go by myself and let him stroll in late? We'd been late for so many things by this point. I'd never seen a bride walk down an aisle, the beginning of a movie, or the opening pitch of one of my girls' softball games. Now my daughter, who had middle-child syndrome anyway, was left sitting in a pew without a family. (This is something she still brings up as a low point in her life, and she's 35 now.)

I decided that I wasn't going to wait for him next time, and I didn't. He came home late for our departure for the next commitment we had, and he was shocked that I'd left. I didn't care, and to this day that's what I do. We don't argue or fight anymore over his tardiness because I just go alone, and he gets there when he gets there. I have to tell you though, as the years have gone by, he's getting to be more punctual. Why? He doesn't like walking in alone.

THE SECOND THING I'VE LEARNED from a lengthy marriage is that screaming gets me nowhere. I hate to admit that this took me years and several sore throats to figure out. In the beginning, my volume did have an impact because he was concerned about who might hear us. There was nothing he tried to avoid more than our neighbors having a front-row seat for our fights. As time passed, however, he saw that I was going to yell and learned to tune out my ranting. It was as though he pressed some internal mute button.

I'll admit that some of the things I yelled about were rather petty. I was young, and the whole marriage thing wasn't exactly what I expected. I thought we were going to be sharing romantic dinners together every night, watch television while cuddling on the couch, and holding hands everywhere we went. About a month after the wedding, I discovered this was a really mistaken assumption.

So when I didn't get my way, I bitched. I hate to use that word, but really, that's the truth of it. If bitching were an Olympic sport, I'd have a slew of gold medals. I complained about everything. I began to notice that there was a correlation between the amount of fussing I did and the amount of time my husband spent at work. I also realized that when I was harping on little things, the really important things got lost.

Little by little, I learned to curb my tongue, and something interesting started to happen. My husband was around more, and he began to listen to my complaints. We were able to discuss things calmly, and the results were much more positive than any I'd gotten with all my bitching.

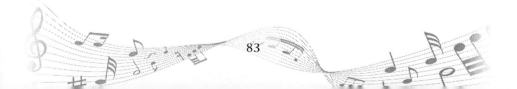

This brings me to my husband's weapon of choice when he's really angry: the silent treatment. He can go days without speaking to me. Because I'm a communicator, this is cruel and unusual punishment. Throughout our marriage, there have been incidents where he gets so angry that he just shuts down. He stops talking and treats me as if I'm invisible. This really hurts.

Each time he did this, rather than getting easier, it got more difficult for me. When he finally decided to talk, he always acted as if nothing had happened. He just wanted to forget the whole thing. It was like a dark cloud formation that stalled over the sun. When it blew over, everything was bright and shiny as if the cloud had never been there.

The last time my husband pulled this, I was out of town. He wouldn't take my calls, and we went three days without speaking. I was frantic, so I cut my trip short and came home to fix things. I wasn't even sure why he was angry, but apparently I'd committed a crime that warranted this punishment. He came home from work and was surprised to find me back early. He gave me a big hug and smiled as if it was the most natural thing in the world.

I hadn't been given the silent treatment in quite a while, so I was baffled by his behavior. Finally, I asked what was wrong, and when he told me I must admit the bitch returned. I screamed my lungs out. I couldn't believe he'd put me through that just because I'd forgotten to fill out some paperwork necessary for re-mortgaging our home.

The bitching was effective because I don't do it that much anymore; and when I calmed down, we talked. I told him in no uncertain terms that I wasn't going to tolerate this behavior any longer. We'd come too far in our marriage, and I'd grown too much as a woman, to put up with it. He agreed that he was overreacting and promised that it wouldn't happen again. I told him that it had better not because I wouldn't put up with it again.

The gauntlet was thrown.

A few months later, we were invited to the wedding of two of my friends that fell on the most sacred of days. No, it wasn't Christmas, but the date of my husband's company picnic. Ever since he's owned this business, that is a sacrosanct day. I've attended every one of these picnics for 25 years, dutifully standing by his side as the owner's wife.

When the invitation came, my first impulse was to immediately say I couldn't go, but then something stopped me. This was something I really wanted to do. It was a huge honor to have been invited, as this wedding was a small, intimate affair. I felt very close to the couple who was being married, and another friend was officiating. I didn't want to miss it. There was no way I could do both things because the wedding was out of town and at the exact same time as the picnic.

I decided to do the unthinkable and discuss this with my husband. He listened attentively as I told him about the invitation and what an honor this was for me. His response was that he would have to think about it.

I put it on the line and said, "If this is something we decide that I do, I'd better not get the silent treatment, because I'm not going through that again."

Eventually, we decided (as a couple) that I should go. I was so proud of my evolved husband actually putting one of my desires ahead of his own. I knew it was difficult for him, and on the way to the airport, I thanked him for his support and understanding. The day of the event arrived, and I was so glad that I was there. It was magical in every sense of the word, and I really wished my husband could have been there to enjoy it with me.

When I called him to share all the details and find out about his picnic, there was no answer. I felt a bit uneasy, but thought maybe he got "tied up" at the picnic. After many more tries, I quit around 11 o'clock that night. There was no doubt in my mind. I was getting the silent treatment.

What was I going to do? I was supposed to be gone for a week because I had business in the same vicinity as the wedding the following weekend. I was going to spend the in-between days with one of my friends. I just knew in my heart that he wasn't going to take my calls or contact me for the entire week. I had thrown down the

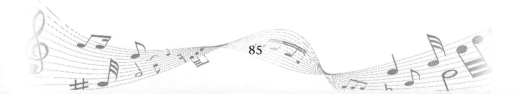

gauntlet, saying that I wouldn't accept such behavior any more. This left one question: *Now what?*

My first impulse was to run home and get things straightened out, but I knew that I couldn't pacify him again. This was totally unfair, and I didn't deserve to be treated like a child. That was my key thought: *I did not deserve this.* At the same time, I knew that if I went to my friend's house, I'd spend all my time looking at my cell phone and explaining my husband's infantile behavior to my friend.

What if I could go away for a few days where I could be incommunicado? I was near a place dear to my heart—Sedona, Arizona— and I could go there and get back in time for my work. There was a fabulous spa there that I'd always wanted to splurge on and, best of all, no cell service. Should I? Could I? Dare I?

Before I could change my mind, I called the spa, plunked down my credit card for a nonrefundable spa package, booked my flight, and explained what was going on to my friend. The next morning, I was on my way with one thought floating through my brain: *Are you really doing this?*

Those three days put me more in touch with myself than anything had done in the past. I was pampered and fed gourmet meals, and I did exactly what I wanted while not worrying about my husband or kids. My job was to please no one but myself. It was freeing to be so anonymous, and even though I usually make friends everywhere, I luxuriated in my solitude.

No one knew where I was except for my friend and my sister, who could contact me in case of an emergency. When I left the gorgeous red rock canyons of Sedona, I was revitalized and renewed. I didn't know where our marriage was going to go, but I did know that whatever happened, I would be fine.

When I got home after one entire week of not speaking, my husband acted as though nothing had happened. I quietly told him that I wasn't accepting that and let him know where I'd been all week. He was astounded to think that I'd gone somewhere new and he'd had no idea where I was. All of a sudden, the tables were turned, and he told me that I'd deserted him.

I just laughed at that. I knew that his big plan of torment had fallen flat, and he couldn't believe that instead of being a pile of mush, I was sparkling with spa glow from head to toe. To date, I haven't endured another silent treatment. And since he saw what his display of temper cost him, prominently displayed on our credit-card bill, I'm sure that one was the last.

I'LL ADMIT THAT I'M NOT THE SAME WOMAN my husband married. I've almost single-handedly raised three daughters, because my husband owns a business and believes he lives there rather than at home. There were times when the girls were young that I'd have to introduce him to his own kids when he showed up for dinner.

I learned along the way that the only thing I could do to survive was to create a life of my own. We were never going to be one of those couples that did everything together. I was lucky to see him in our bed at night. Anything else was a bonus.

Did I ever consider divorce? Yes. Would I be better off with someone else—maybe someone I had more in common with? Perhaps I could find someone who enjoyed walking on the beach and didn't complain that the sand irritated his feet? My dream man would like to watch new shows on TV or a foreign film once in a while instead of the same movies over and over again. I've seen *Crimson Tide* so many times with him that I'm sure I could serve on a nuclear submarine. But something told me that divorce wasn't the answer.

All in all, he's a good guy and there was one stumbling block to divorce: I truly loved this man. I knew that the void I was trying to get him to fill was one I could address myself, so I opted for a more conservative approach and found enjoyable ways to fill my time.

On this path, I've always had a job that I felt passionate about. Although they were all part-time since being a mom was my top priority, I always worked at a position that was enjoyable. My résumé was long, but whether I was teaching aerobics or meditation workshops, I always treasured what I did.

I also found a place to live that I truly loved, the one I've described on Sanibel Island in Florida. First, this was a vacation home, and then a part-time residence. It was all with my husband's full

approval, as he saw Sanibel as our retirement destination. He was all for it . . . at least in the beginning.

I think he liked his bachelor days when I was out of town, with no one to answer to, and I loved the freedom. All my daughters had moved out, two with families of their own; and although my youngest did come back at times, for the most part the nest was empty. I was liberated, shedding my stay-at-home mom role. For the first time in my life, I was living as an independent woman. I could eat what I wanted, when I wanted; go to bed with a good book instead of a TV blaring in the background; and answer to no one but myself.

What a wonderful feeling . . . but something happened along the way. The more used to being self-sufficient I got, the more my husband discovered that he didn't like it that much. He began to get lonely and tell me that he missed me.

By this time, we had a house on Sanibel, which he insisted on buying because he hated sharing a swimming pool in the condo development where we'd been living. I told him that if we bought the house, it meant that I'd have to spend more time there. It was much more responsibility; and with no condo manager to oversee things, it would all fall on me.

"Don't worry," he said. "In the next few years, I'll retire, and then we'll have this house to live in. Until then, you enjoy yourself."

He was changing the rules, and I didn't know what to do. The fluidity of our marriage river was shifting.

I didn't want to spend more time in cold and snowy New York because I had new friends and more of a life in Florida. Plus I could get my kids and "Nonni" fixes over long weekends there and they loved to visit the sunshine whenever they could.

But what would I do about my husband? He tried to visit, but it just wasn't enough. Going back and forth left me feeling like the Energizer Bunny with the wrong brand of battery, about to run out of juice. I had clothes here, there, and everywhere; I had friends here, there, and everywhere. I had a life here, there, and everywhere.

It was time for my husband and me to evolve again, and we needed to talk about what was going on. Men always seem to love "the talks," and mine is no exception. He did his famous eye roll at my suggestion and tried to put it off to a better time.

I told him there was no better time and that we had to discuss where our marriage was going. We were beginning to live totally separate lives, and I felt this was a dangerous situation. At a time when we should be on the same page, we weren't even in the same book.

We went out for dinner at one of our favorite getaway places. The atmosphere makes us feel romantic just walking through the door. We snagged our favorite booth, sat next to each other, and really began to discuss our situation. I started the ball rolling, of course, but I'm happy to say that he actively participated.

Compromises were called for, and we came up with a plan. It would mean a bit more traveling for both of us, but it was something that we could both make work. We also agreed that eventually Florida would be our home base, and this made me happiest of all.

I WAS HEADING BACK TO FLORIDA right after spending the Thanksgiving holiday in New York. My husband and I agreed to take this trip together, but at the last minute he couldn't make it due to a work conflict. I was a bit put out because it seemed as though he was already starting to mess with our plan, so I let him know as much.

He promised that he'd make it up to me. On the way to the airport, he was giddy with excitement and said, "Wait till you see the surprise I have planned for you this year. It's going to be your best Christmas!"

I must be honest and say that after some of the surprises of Christmases past, this statement struck terror in my heart. First of all, the fact that he had an idea right after Thanksgiving startled me completely. The Christmas Eve–shopper extraordinaire was thinking about my gift already? What could this mean?

As we were driving, I glanced at him and caught him grinning in a way similar to Jack Nicholson when he says, "Here's Johnny!" in *The Shining*. I began to get scared, but all he'd say was "You are going to be so surprised!"

Upon my return in the first week of December, my husband picked me up at the airport and seemed to be back to normal. As

we rounded the corner of our block, I noticed a house all decorated brilliantly with white lights, sparkling from top to bottom. It was breathtaking, beautiful and festive with a majestic evergreen tree that stood in the yard, twinkling brightly—at least 12 feet of Christmas splendor.

Wait a minute . . . it was our house!

"Surprise!" my husband yelled. I couldn't believe it. Ever since I was a child, I'd longed for a house decorated this way, and it was truly a dream come true. With tears in my eyes, I hugged and kissed him and then said a deep-felt thank-you. My husband had finally "seen the light."

IN THESE DAYS, WHEN ONE OUT of two marriages ends in divorce, I'm proud of the fact that we've survived more than 40 years. I've kept my family together, and we've served as good role models for my daughters in their marriages. They've seen us with all our warts and know that we've worked hard to stay together.

Recently, my husband was a guest on my Internet radio show. The title of this episode was "You Found Your Soul Mate . . . Now What?" The fact that he agreed to be on my show was a feat in itself, but when a listener called in and asked him what he felt made our marriage work he said, "My wife is the first person I want to see in the morning and the last person I want to see at night."

That short comment was worth a thousand words. It was so perfectly put; and as I thought about it, I realized that in every sense of the word, this man that I met so long ago at an amusement park is now my best friend in the world.

Is there anything better than that?

🔲 🔲 🔲

CHAPTER 10

Take a Walk
on the Wild Side

My husband was driving me to the airport when we got into one of our heated debates—or maybe it was more of an inquisition. I was on my way to Santa Fe, New Mexico, to spend a few days with a woman I didn't know very well and my husband didn't know at all.

"Where are you staying?" he asked.

He always likes to have the name of my hotel, which I feel is a reasonable request but amusing to me, since there have been times when he left on a business trip and I didn't even know what state he'd be sleeping in that night.

"I don't know," I answered.

"What?!" he shouted. "How could you not know where you're staying?"

"She's been there many times before, and she made all the ar-rangements," I explained.

To be honest, this was kind of nice for me because I'm usually the one to make all the plans. How fun was it not to worry about the details and just enjoy the ride? Naturally, my husband didn't see it that way and seemed positively astounded. He gave me one of his infamous head shakes and looked at me as though I were a pre-schooler climbing into a strange car after being offered a candy bar.

"I like the idea of just going," I defended myself. "At least it won't be boring."

"One thing I can honestly say about you is that in the last few years, you've never been boring," he responded.

Wait—was that a compliment? Note: Ask Dr. Phil.

By this point, we'd arrived at the airport and his comment was hanging in the air. I kissed him good-bye, promised I'd call with all the details, and hurried to catch my plane. His nagging doubts were actually beginning to have an impact on me, and I wanted to make a hasty retreat before that negativity put a damper on my excitement about the unknown.

As I sat waiting for takeoff, I thought more about his comment. Was it true that I'd crossed over from being the predictable wife and mom to someone who was willing to try new things? As I grew older had I actually become—dare I say it—adventuresome? *Wow,* I thought. *I've come a long way, baby!* I felt that his comment truly was a compliment.

Not long before, I was working in Hawaii and decided to go swimming with the dolphins. When the boat arrived to pick us up, it was nothing more than a glorified raft. I looked at the woman who'd organized this swim and asked her if this were merely a dinghy, taking us to our real boat, which I assumed would be the size of an ocean liner—or a million-dollar yacht, at the very least.

She just smiled, thinking that I was joking, which led me to the quick realization this dinky boat was actually the only thing preventing us from drowning. Yes, it was our only transportation. I love the water, so I quickly adjusted—and had one of the most incredible experiences of my life, swimming with a pod of dolphins in the deep blue Pacific. I'll never forget the songs they sang or the mother and baby moving majestically below me. There were dolphins surrounding me on all sides, and tears filled my swimming mask as I felt at one with their beauty and energy.

Maybe this was risky by my husband's standards, but it's something I wouldn't have wanted to miss. Yes, I'd take his crack as high praise, and I was smiling as the plane took off.

My flight arrived in Albuquerque right on schedule, and my friend picked me up and took me to the bed-and-breakfast where we were staying in Santa Fe. How lovely to have had all these plans made for me, and the inn was charming. Although we didn't know each other well, I felt that her choice of accommodations showed we had a great deal in common. I was a bit tired from the trip but got caught up in her enthusiasm as she showed me the charms of this quaint city.

As we were walking into town, my friend told me that there was a fantastic spa where she'd like to take me the next day. Would I like a massage?

Does Sarah Palin like to hunt?

My tired muscles tingled at the thought, and I said, "Sure."

Quickly, she made us spa appointments and excitedly told me that I was going to love this place.

"There's an amazing hot tub there. It's outdoors, and all you see are the mountains and trees. Clothing is optional. You'll love the freedom of being naked in the hot water with the cool breeze caressing your body," she breathlessly told me.

Really? I thought. *Naked?* And then I reminded myself, *I'm not boring, not boring, not boring.*

Let me digress here and tell you how I know this woman. She's a personal trainer at my gym, and she does Pilates every day. There is not one fat cell on her body—even her toes look muscular. As much as I had little problem soaking naked in the hot tubs of the Bellagio in Las Vegas, that was with people I didn't know and would never see again, or could certainly duck into a bathroom to avoid. I couldn't imagine being nude in front of this paragon of fitness.

"Sounds great," I fibbed. In true Scarlett O'Hara fashion, I figured that I'd worry about this—and my naked thighs—tomorrow.

All too soon, tomorrow came. Off we went to the spa, and it was indeed located on the top of a sublimely beautiful mountain. Upon arrival, we were given kimonos befitting the Japanese atmosphere. Each one had a Japanese symbol painted on the back. I quickly noticed that my friend had a turquoise symbol, while mine was black. Insecurity already setting in, I decided these characters probably stood for "petite" (hers) and "elephantine" (mine).

How am I ever going to do this? I wondered, knowing that I couldn't be totally naked in front of a woman I might even see at Target after our trip was over.

Just as we were going up to the tub, my friend said that she had to use the restroom. Seizing my chance, I told her that I'd meet her up there, ran up about 1,000 Japanese-style steps, rushed into the

tub area, ripped off my robe, and practically cannonballed into the hot tub. Yay! I beat her! First crisis averted.

Allowing myself to relax for the first time, I looked around and noticed all the naked women staring at me. Some were in the tub, and some were lying on chaises around it. They were all very quiet, with the only sound being the rustle of the glorious evergreen trees around us. I realized my entrance had broken their serene environment, and I sheepishly smiled an apology.

At that moment, my friend walked in, quietly disrobed, and entered the water like Aphrodite.

Forgive me as I digress here once again. When did it become a custom to style one's pubic hair? As I looked around, pretending to not really be looking, the first thing I noticed was all the styles of pubic hair adorning these women. There were the Mohawk, the beard, the landing strip, and even the baldy.

The first time I'd been exposed to this was when I saw my youngest daughter coming out of the shower and realized she was totally shaved. I was horrified.

"What happened to your . . . your . . . ," I stammered as I pointed to her pubic region.

"I shaved it," she responded, rolling her eyes. "It's gross any other way, and you should really do something about that landscaping of yours. It looks like an overgrown bunch of petunias in the garden."

I was speechless. All I could l think of was how uncomfortable it was when that "area" was shaved for me before I gave birth to my daughters. Now they were doing this as some kind of fashion statement. Did they learn about this on *Sex and the City*? Was it on the pages of *Vogue* under "Hot Spring Styles"? I'd certainly heard of Brazilian waxing, but I'd assumed that was only for people who lived in Brazil, and maybe Kim Cattrall's character, Samantha. Apparently, once again I'd missed the latest trend.

Let's go back to the naked hot tub—or the let-it-all-hang-out soak. After some time, the water was feeling pretty hot, and I was beginning to look like one of those wrinkled apple sculptures. I had to make my escape, and when I looked for my friend, I noticed that she was lying on a chaise with her eyes closed. Luck was with me. I stepped out of the tub and found the nearest chaise, discreetly covering myself with a towel. Finally relaxed, I took a deep breath of mountain air. Incredible.

Just then, a lovely girl of about 30 walked in. She was your basic nightmare: a nubile nymph with a perfect body. We exchanged smiles, and she gracefully entered the hot tub. I looked at the leaves of the trees above me, glowing in the sun, closed my eyes, and began to meditate.

Just then, I heard a noise very close by. I opened my eyes, and right there, the nubile nymph was doing the yoga move downward-facing dog in all her naked glory. The rear end of the dog was directly in front of me. (For those of you who don't know yoga poses, picture an inverted *V* with hands and feet on the floor, butt pushed to the sky.)

I quickly closed my eyes again, feeling that I was invading her privacy, but not quite believing what I'd just seen. This was taking "free spirit" to a whole new level in more ways than one. I peeked again and found that she was doing lunges and stretches, each one more provocative than the next. I also noticed that quite a few of the women were now discreetly watching this show. Finally, she sat in a cross-legged position to meditate with a towel covering her lap. Score one for modesty! Her mother would have been proud!

I figured she was finished, so I closed my eyes once again and heard the rustle of her towel. Little did I know that she'd saved the best for last! I opened my eyes as my name was being called to go for my massage. There she was, doing a pose that I'm sure only her gynecologist had seen up until that point. She was flat on her back, feet together, and legs wide open. Nothing was left up to the imagination. I quickly averted my eyes and left the tub area. (In case you're wondering . . . she was wearing a Mohawk.)

Our treatments were heavenly, and I enjoyed the rest of the day immensely. As we were leaving, I asked my friend if the show we saw at the hot tub was a normal occurrence. Maybe once again there was a fad that I was the last to know about: naked yoga. That wasn't the

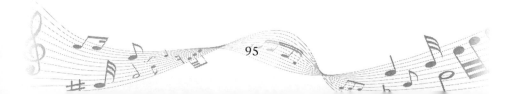

case, however. She assured me that she'd been there numerous times and had never seen anything like that.

IN BED THAT NIGHT, I THOUGHT about the entire experience. I was really glad I hadn't let my fear of being seen by my friend in my naked glory stop me from enjoying that hot tub. It was an extraordinary experience and so liberating to be nude in the great outdoors.

To let go of all the trappings of the material world and bare all—well, it isn't boring. To really allow myself to be seen, and to see, for that matter, was invigorating. Maybe that was the message from the nubile nymph. Obviously free of any inhibitions, she allowed herself to open up on all levels. She was free in every sense of the word and obviously didn't care about what anyone thought. Maybe it was time for me to really take a walk on the wild side and try one of those Mohawks!

Or maybe I could just work on letting my towel drop for 30 seconds . . . in my own tub . . . with the window open.

It's a start.

⊞ ⊞ ⊞

CHAPTER 11

His Way

In March two years ago, I was driving my husband to the airport in Florida after we'd spent a lovely weekend together. He was retuning to New York, and just as we were pulling in, I noticed that I had a missed call on my cell phone. It was from my brother, who'd been undergoing medical tests that day to see if the chemotherapy treatments he was receiving were working.

"You better call him back," my husband said.

"I'll drop you off first." I replied.

"I think you should do it now," he pressed.

I agreed and placed the call, and my brother answered on the first ring. His voice was raspy, and he sounded exhausted. Each time I spoke to him, he sounded more like a living ghost. I could tell by his tone that he was getting weaker and weaker.

"Sue, they've given me two weeks to live," he said.

These words reverberated in my head with an energy all their own. Two weeks? How was that even possible? Random thoughts raced through my mind.

"What do I tell Mom?" he asked. How could I answer that? What do you say to someone you love as dearly as I loved my brother when he receives news that he has 14 days to live? It was impossible to comprehend. It was typical of his personality that although he was sick, he was more worried about our mother.

"Wait," I told him. "I'm coming home as soon as I can get a flight. We'll deal with this together."

"You don't have to do that. It really isn't necessary," he said and by this point his voice was shaking with the immensity of the situation that was facing him.

"No arguing. I am coming home. I can help you with this, but you have to let me see you," I insisted.

"Okay."

"How do you feel? Is there anything I can do now?" I asked.

It was quiet for a moment, and then he said, "I just can't believe that in two weeks' time, I will not be here. I won't be with my wife and my family. They will sit and watch TV without me. I can't believe I will not be here."

I didn't try to diminish the enormity of this with platitudes.

"This sucks!" I said, knowing it was best to just be honest and sincere. "I will be there for you and do whatever I can. And I'm still holding out for a miracle. . . . Love you."

"Love you," he replied, hanging up.

For a moment, the silence was profound. In two weeks, all there would be was silence.

My husband had been circling the airport while I talked on the phone. I told him that he wouldn't be catching his plane because I had to get a flight to New York as soon as possible, and I was in no shape to do it by myself.

There were things I had to take care of at home there in Florida before I could leave, so we started back to the house. Then something happened that I couldn't explain. Without any warning, a soul-wrenching, primal scream was released from my lungs. Then I kicked the dashboard and railed at the God I'd so fervently been praying to.

I sobbed and yelled, "How could you let this happen?!"

I did this as I shook my fist to the heavens. We were in a convertible, so quite a few people witnessed this outburst, but I didn't care. The emotions inside me were savage and raw and couldn't be suppressed.

My husband didn't try to quiet me. He let me howl away my pain like a wounded animal. By time we got home, I was exhausted. Emotionally, mentally, and spiritually, I was spent. I found a flight that left first thing the next morning, and we went to bed.

I didn't sleep a wink that night. I thought back to the last time I saw my brother. We were both busy with careers and families and only saw each other on holidays and family events. The most recent had been at my newest granddaughter's christening in November. He looked robust then, and we had a great time at the party.

I learned later that he'd been feeling lousy due to stomach problems, but I wasn't worried. He'd always had a sensitive stomach, so this wasn't unusual, and there were no red flags to think it was anything serious.

By Christmas, though, he was feeling so ill that he couldn't attend any of the family festivities. I started to worry, and the tests began. On New Year's Eve, the diagnosis came in: stomach cancer. The prognosis: terminal.

That night I got very drunk. The next day, I talked to my brother, and I told him not to give up. Miracles happened all the time. Look at Lance Armstrong. He promised me that he wouldn't quit. He wanted to live. He had a wife and children, and he wasn't ready to leave his family.

The chemo began, and the side effects were so bad that I couldn't believe a human being could endure them. Each time he was tested to see if the treatment was being effective, the results were the same: no change. Here it was March, and his latest tests indicated that there was no use in putting his body through any more of this torture. There was no more that could be done.

I talked to him often during this time, but he used every excuse in the book not to get together. My father had passed away from cancer five years earlier, and every time I asked to visit my brother, he told me, "I look just like Dad did."

My brother had lost a great deal of weight and didn't want me seeing him looking sickly. I honored that request, but now I couldn't. In my heart, I knew time was running out. As much as I continued to pray for a miracle, I just wanted his suffering to end.

I FLEW BACK TO BUFFALO AND PLANNED to see my brother the next day. I didn't tell my mother I was in town because I didn't want to alert her to the seriousness of the situation. I wanted to see my brother first.

I will admit there was a part of me that was still in denial and was nervous about seeing him. I knew that once I did, there would be no way I could pretend that all this wasn't really happening. But there was no time for further delays or diversion tactics. My brother had

called, and I felt that he needed me to be a big sister and help him with the biggest challenge he'd ever face. I wouldn't let him down.

As I drove to his house, all I did was pray for the courage and the strength not to fall apart when I saw him. I knew that he'd look vastly different from the last time we were together, and having so recently witnessed cancer's death pallor on my father, I couldn't imagine seeing it on my younger brother.

His wife had taken a leave of absence from her job and was taking care of him. She'd created a sacred environment in their home for his passing. When I walked through the door, I felt the unconditional love of a wife taking care of her dying husband. Through the next few days of his illness, she never left his side. The care she gave my brother is something I will always remember as the highest example of selfless love.

As much as I tried to prepare myself for this meeting, there was no way to be ready. My brother was a handsome man who wore his Italian heritage proudly, including bright brown eyes, wavy brown hair, and a full mustache. He had just enough of a belly to let you know that he enjoyed his pasta and wine. He was a fine cook, and his meals were legendary.

The man I saw that day was still my brother; but when I looked at him, I saw his essence, not his physical reality. He was so thin, and his skin tone had taken on a yellow tinge indicative of liver failure. He looked me in the eyes, and I knew that he wanted to see reassurance. He wanted to see in my gaze that he didn't seem that bad. I am proud to say my eyes reflected back to him exactly what I saw.

I saw the little boy who used to ride bikes and swim with me on hot summer days. I saw all the adventures we had in the empty fields near our house where we hunted for frogs and tadpoles. He was my childhood, and that's what I was gazing upon. I smiled at him, and I knew my whole face lit up.

Finally he asked me, "Don't I look like Dad did?"

"You look like an Italian lover who should be sitting in a restaurant in Rome, sipping a fine red wine and dipping fresh bread in olive oil," I replied, sitting down next to him.

I couldn't stop hugging him. If I could have pulled him inside me at that point and taken away all his pain, I would have. He began to whisper in my ear and tell me what he wanted for his funeral arrangements.

I listened without reacting, knowing that more than anything, he needed me to be strong. He was concerned about his wife and family. His oldest daughter from his first marriage, now in her 20s, had just lost her mother to cancer a year before. His second marriage had produced two beautiful children: a girl, 15, and a boy, 13. What was to become of them without a father?

I reassured him and promised that his family would be fine. He could rest peacefully on that count. All of us would see to it.

Looking back on this conversation, I don't know how I held it together. At times like that, all we can do is pull from a pool of strength that we never knew we possessed. Falling apart just wasn't a luxury I had that day.

I told him that I'd take care of telling Mom, and he could rest easy on that one as well. We held each other, and then he cried. I felt that he was releasing the last bit of himself.

I LEFT THERE WITH THE INTENTION of heading directly to my mother's house. Just as I was pulling out of my brother's driveway, the phone rang—and it was my mom.

"You have to get right back to New York! Your brother is in bad shape," she told me in a panicked voice.

"I'm already here, Mom, and I'll be right there," I replied.

As luck would have it, my niece had told her maternal grandmother the severity of my brother's condition. She then called my mother, a friend of hers, to offer her support. My mom was in a total state of disbelief and couldn't wrap her head around just how ill my brother was. I let her have her doubts, and she planned to see him the next day with my sister. She was able to say her good-byes then, although to the very end, she still felt he would get better.

DURING THAT TIME, HOSPICE CARE came in to make my brother as comfortable as possible. I went over every day, armed with my sister-in-law's favorite latte. There were times when she was up to company, and I came in. Other days, when she wasn't up to seeing anyone, I delivered her coffee and left. By this time, my brother was in a coma.

I knew that hearing is the last sense to go, so on one of my visits, I decided to remind him of a story from our childhood.

"Do you remember that time we got stuck in the mud?" I asked him.

Silence.

It had been a really rainy spring in Buffalo that year, and we always cut through a vacant lot on our way home from school to shorten our walk. On that day, it looked like a sea of quicksand.

"Let's go for it," he said.

So we did. About halfway through the lot, neither of us could lift our feet anymore. Our shoes were coated with mud, and they got heavier and heavier with each step, until finally we couldn't move at all. We were seriously stuck.

The only solution we could come up with was to take our shoes off. Both of us knew there would be hell to pay with our father, but we had no choice. We stepped out of our shoes and walked the rest of the way home in our socks. I've often thought of those two pairs of shoes stuck there for all time and what people thought when they saw them.

Telling the story made me laugh, and I felt the energy in the room shift. I knew that he heard me and was laughing right along with me. I don't recall what exactly did happen when we got home, but it couldn't have been too bad. What a great story I was able to share with him.

ON A SATURDAY, THERE WAS A BENEFIT for my brother arranged by his co-workers. He had many careers, most notably as a bartender and bar owner, but in his 40s he went back to school and became a psychiatric nurse. This was his proudest achievement. I've been to many of these benefit events before, but I can honestly say that

I've never seen so many people at one. They remembered him from all times of his life, and everyone shared smiles and tears as they recounted stories with him as the main character.

As a traveling nurse, his patients were primarily geriatric, and many of them couldn't afford their medications. His boss told us all that on those occasions, my brother paid for their prescriptions out of his own pocket, a practice he could ill afford. This was only one example of how he touched others' lives. I could feel the love in the room and realized what an extraordinary man my brother had become. I was so proud to be his sister.

The Wednesday night after the benefit, I was especially restless. I hadn't been sleeping well throughout this ordeal, but no matter how hard I tried that night, I just couldn't get comfortable. Then all of a sudden, I found myself gasping for breath. It was a weird sensation, and I wasn't frightened—just puzzled. Finally, my breathing settled down, and the phone rang.

It was my niece telling me that my brother, Thomas Edward Kobza, had died. I felt my breathing distress was tied to his last gasps of life. He died peacefully, and his wife and oldest daughter were by his side. He'd said good-bye to his other children, and they were sleeping upstairs when he passed away. I think he wanted to spare them the final moments.

I rushed over to say my final good-byes, but I knew he'd left a long time before I got there. This shell he left behind—that we all leave behind—was just that, a shell.

THE FUNERAL PLANS WERE ALL in place, and I'm blessed to have a friend in the business. My sister-in-law, my niece, and I went to make the final arrangements. Cost was a concern, so my friend began to tell us of a way to save on a major ticket item. He explained that they had beautiful coffins that were used for display, then deeply discounted and like brand-new. The more he used the word *display* the more our antennas went up.

"Do you mean the display models in the showroom?" I asked.

"No I'm talking about caskets that we use to display people that are being cremated. They're totally cleaned, of course," he explained.

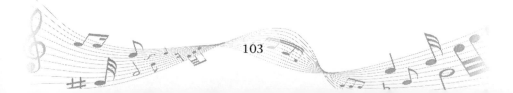

"A used casket!" my sister-in-law gasped. "Tom would never forgive me for that."

This struck us all as so funny that we began to laugh and couldn't stop. My brother was generous to a fault and lived abundantly, whether he could afford to or not. There was no way he would understand or condone any "used coffin" for his final resting place. So we purchased a sparkling new one and were on our way, still chuckling.

HIS SERVICE TWO DAYS LATER was just what he'd wanted. I made sure that all of his requests were honored. Tom had asked that the casket be closed, but the funeral director strongly suggested we have a private viewing as a family. He said that those who didn't see their loved ones usually regretted it. My sister-in-law agreed, and we were all glad that we had an opportunity to see Tom looking like his old self. He truly did appear to be sleeping, and at any moment I expected him to sit up and offer us all a beer.

At the service, I was in shock to think that it truly was all over—and much too soon. My brother had passed on April 1, not even living the last two weeks he was promised. My husband sat next to me and held my hand, and I was so thankful that he'd been a huge source of comfort and support to me throughout this process. He respected my needs, and when I craved silence, he left me alone. When I wanted to talk, he let me chatter without interruption. When I had no more to give, he convinced me that I had just a bit more. When I couldn't go on, I drew from his well of love.

My mother sat on my other side. She's a short woman to begin with, and she looked to me as though she'd actually shrunk even more over the last week. Losing a child is a mother's worst nightmare, and I couldn't fathom the deep recesses of her pain. She was in her 80s, which should have been a time of stress-free retirement. Yet there she was, dealing with tragedy. I respect that until the end, my mother never gave up hope. Her faith is what kept her standing. As a mother, I knew this was something she'd survive, but never get over.

I thought about my brother and me as children and how well we knew each other. It saddened me to think that we hadn't taken the time to know each other better as adults. I'm still discovering things about him that I never knew. Sure, there were the holidays and family gatherings, but our busy schedules dictated our time, and we didn't make the space for a long chat . . . just the two of us, just to see how we were both doing. Holidays were a monumental effort, and we had to rush to catch up while making sure that everyone was happy, eating, talking, and getting along. There just wasn't enough time.

There had been petty differences, too, that in hindsight seemed too insignificant to even really remember. I wished that I had a rewind button and could also stop, pause, and then stage a "do over." Doesn't everyone wish for that at some point?

I knew that the things that I'd learned from this experience were profound. I knew that there are no certainties in life, especially when it comes to the people we love. It was clear that I could never tell someone "I love you" enough. I understood that a childhood spent together creates a bond that's never broken.

I realized that from the moment he passed away, I'd never stop missing my brother.

It brought me comfort to know that Tom lived his life his way. He knew how to celebrate with the best of them, and his party life was legendary. I could picture him on the Other Side with my Dad, sharing a fine Chianti and a dish of spaghetti. Tom left behind an amazing family and a legacy of compassion and generosity. I smiled, thinking about this accomplishment. My brother lived a full life. It was much too short, but it was a life well lived.

As I walked out of the service, I thought that I didn't mind aging and the years passing—or should I say flying—by me. There were things about it that I truly enjoyed, but in the last few years, I'd lost people that I cared deeply about, including family and friends. I knew that this was a part of growing older that I could do without, but it was inevitable. It's life.

I looked around at Tom's family and mine and knew that nothing from that point on would stop me from knowing the people I loved intimately, and I would never hold back that extra embrace.

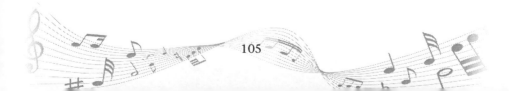

There are moments now when I wish that I could reach out to my brother and feel him just one more time. Not a day goes by that I don't think of him and hold him dearly in my heart.

Is there someone in your life who needs to be hugged today?

❖ ❖ ❖

CHAPTER 12

A Few of My Favorite Things

We all have those days—days when we wish we could just go back to bed, or at the very least hide under it. Unfortunately, that's not often a possibility, so I'd like to share one more song with you: a few of my favorite things. I've found that these little respites from daily life give me a boost when I need it most; I actually schedule "me time" into my iPhone, along with other essential appointments. I then splurge on one of my favorite things. I've learned that it's important to take the time to revitalize myself, body and soul. Each of the activities I mention here does just that, and whether I take an hour or a day, they're key to my well-being.

However, there's one favorite thing I do more consistently than any other, and that's meditation. I consider it an essential part of my day and feel as though something is missing if I skip it. Just as not brushing my teeth can lead to bad breath, I feel that when I don't meditate, my brain gets a little stinky. This time clears out the gunk and helps me start my day with a mind that's cleansed and refreshed. I've actually trademarked a technique called InPowering Meditation™ that I feel takes my daily practice to a whole new level.

So without further discussion, here are a few of my favorite things. They're to change your day from lousy to lovely. (Don't hate me if that *Sound of Music* song won't stop playing in your head now.)

Enjoy . . .

Spa Day

There's nothing more nurturing than the physical touch. Wait—stop thinking about *that*. When I want to feel good all over, I head out to get a massage. Sometimes I want the light touch of a Swedish technique, and other times I need the more aggressive deep tissue approach. Essential oils or hot rocks complement any treatment. When it's done, I feel just delicious all over.

I've found that I can pamper myself for a day without going to some costly resort. I designate a day when I'm "leaving town" and drive to one of my local day spas. I try to find the places where I get the most bang for my buck, such as a workout facility, steam room, or sauna, all included in the price of a manicure, pedicure, or facial.

With a little research, it's amazing the gems you may find in your own backyard. These places often offer deals during the week when they're not so busy, so you can have your getaway without emptying your wallet.

Reading a Great Book

I find that when I need to totally escape, nothing takes me away like a good book. I love all types of literature—everything from Stephen King to Mark Twain. Sometimes a "chick" book fills the bill or a juicy mystery. Reading takes me to worlds that I get to explore and enjoy from the comfort of my chair.

Enjoying a Steamy Hot Beverage

I love brewing a wonderful cup of tea in a pretty teapot with a matching teacup and sipping it slowly, savoring every minute. I also enjoy a luscious latte sprinkled with cinnamon, with foam that creates a mustache on my upper lip. (Cinnamon is also a great way to level out your blood sugar and stop cravings!) Whichever I choose, I find that it's a wonderful break to give myself every day. This is a little slice of "me time" when I just stay in the moment.

Soaking in a Hot Tub

Oh, how I enjoy soaking in a hot tub. As I ease into the water, I always let out a sigh of absolute pleasure. I'll sometimes add sea salt to my bath and create a bit of the ocean for myself, and I also use aromatic oils and candles to enhance the experience. I love the added benefit of being in a tub with whirlpool jets. The pulsating water soothes my tired muscles. *Ahhh . . .* talk about luxury!

Walking

Nothing refreshes me like a long walk. I'm not talking about power walking, but a slow, mindful stroll. Regardless of whether I'm crunching over the snow in Buffalo or sunning on the beach in Sanibel, the sheer pleasure of movement is a delight. I play a game where I focus on my surroundings as much as possible by paying attention to my five senses. It's amazing the vibrancy everything takes on when I'm really present. There's almost a supernatural effect when I ask myself: *What am I seeing? Feeling? Hearing? Smelling?* I've found that when I focus on my sense of taste, the air actually has a flavor all its own. For instance, on a snowy winter day in Buffalo, I experience a cold, icy zing dancing on my tongue; and in Sanibel, it's the heady flavor of the humid, salty air.

Gal-Pal Time

Whether going for a cup of coffee, happy hour, or a meal, I really enjoy the company of my girlfriends. I'm blessed that at this point in my life, I have balanced friendships with like-minded people. We can tell each other anything and everything without any fear of being judged. I love being with these women as we discuss what's going on in our lives with all the joys and challenges. Many of my friends aren't local, so I've discovered the fun of video chatting on the computer. We get a glass of wine or that steamy hot beverage of our choice, and it's almost as good as being in each other's company physically.

Swimming

I'm a water baby. I love to swim in a pool, or better yet in the warm salt water of an ocean. I've swum with dolphins and body-surfed in waves taller than I am. The freedom I feel is indescribable. Nothing rekindles the child in me like feeling water around me. Whether I float or breaststroke, I enjoy each and every sensation.

Riding My Vespa

Yes, as I mentioned in Chapter 8, I have a Vespa—a bright pink one! It's my own little Italian motor scooter that my husband assured me I'd kill myself on. I actually bought it for myself as a birthday gift. I have a matching pink helmet and am known as the Pink Bomber of Sanibel Island. Motoring up to 40 miles an hour with the wind whipping all around me, I feel like Jack Nicholson on that big motorcycle in *Easy Rider*. It's exhilarating and liberating, and it releases the wild thing in me.

Dancing

Put on some music with a great beat, and I'm the first one on the dance floor. I love to shake my booty and wiggle my hips. This is one of the few times I move with creative abandon and don't care who's watching. At weddings, my husband has nicknamed my daughters and me "the Dancing Kobzas," a reference to my maiden name. My father was king of the Dancing Kobzas, and no single lady was safe in his path when my mother was tired and he was searching for a dance partner. One time at a banquet hall where more than one wedding was going on, we actually found him dancing up a storm in another party because he felt the music was better there. Sometimes, when I'm alone, I'll put great music on and move for the soul of it. Nothing frees me quite so much.

Meditation

As I said at the beginning of this chapter, I practice meditation each and every day. Before I reach for medicine to curb my anxiety or help me sleep, or coffee to wake me up, I meditate. It's an easy solution that provides countless benefits.

Sometimes I just light an aromatic candle, get the water flowing in the little fountain I have, and focus on my breath. On days when I can't sit still, I go for a mindful walk that becomes a moving meditation as I stroll slowly and savor all the sights around me. Other times, I use a guided-meditation CD, and there are plenty to choose from. I've recorded my own for the public, called *Butterfly Blessings.*

Meditating isn't complicated, and you don't have to move to India and give up all your earthly possessions to make it be a beneficial part of the day. Let me explain: This doesn't have to be anything mystical or intimidating. Simply put, it's a way to calm yourself from the inside out. It's all about letting go—no straining, just allowing. There are no goals, and it's best not to have preconceived notions about what's going to happen.

I find that the people who have the most difficult time are those with high expectations, even to the point of being fearful. I can assure you that you won't go to parts unknown and be unable to return. You won't have an experience similar to being on LSD. Most of the time, you'll just reach a level of profound relaxation; and once that becomes a part of your day, the benefits you derive will be incredible.

Here's a simple method you can use to get started:

— First and foremost, create your environment. Make sure that you're somewhere you won't be disturbed. Put the phone away and dedicate this time to yourself. I like to have an aromatic candle burning, my water fountain flowing, and soothing music playing in the background. The important thing here is to make your surroundings as relaxing as possible.

— Once that's set, get in a position that will be comfortable for 10 to 20 minutes. It isn't necessary to be contorted into some kind of pretzel. Find a pose that's relaxing and beneficial for you. I like to sit on a large pillow designed for meditation, with my back straight and my knees in a cross-legged position. If my knees aren't cooperating that day, then I sit in a cozy chair or in my bed with my back supported by pillows and my legs straight out in front of me. Lying down is also an option, with a pillow under your knees and one for your head. I find personally that this invites me to sleep, so I prefer to sit, but whatever works for you is fine.

— Once you're comfortable, gently close your eyes. You're going to begin what's called "belly breathing." Slowly take a deep inhalation, and when you do, bring the breath down deep into your midsection. When you do this correctly, you can feel your stomach expand.

Once you've inhaled completely, slowly exhale, beginning with the belly. Do this four to five times, feeling the air softly coming in and going out. With each breath, notice your body getting more and more relaxed.

— Your mind is going to wander, and the key is to not get carried away with your thoughts, especially those that worry you. When you feel the concerns creeping in, gently bring yourself back to your breath and focus on the inhale . . . and exhale.

— If you're concerned about knowing how much time has passed, there are a few things you can do. One option is simply to have a clock close by. Note the time you start, then when you feel ready to end your meditation, open one eye and peek to see if your instinct is accurate. There are also clocks that have nature sounds, and you could set a soothing alarm to "wake" you after 10 to 20 minutes. You'll find a method that works, and you'll be surprised by the fact that the more you meditate, the more you'll just know when your time is up.

One thing to remember is that you should bring yourself back to your physical surroundings kindly and serenely. When you've been in such a relaxed state, you don't want to be startled back to reality. Be sure that's not a possibility.

— As far as how long to meditate, there are no minimums and maximums. I advise 10 minutes at the beginning, working up to 20 minutes, but you can certainly go longer. There's also no perfect time of day, just the one that's best for you. I like to practice first thing in the morning before I start my day, but sometimes on a busy morning I'll wait until the evening. I also meditate during the day if I need something to calm me down.

— As with any practice, the more you do it, the better you'll get. No matter how experienced you are, though, there will be days that it just seems impossible to sit still, and all you can think about is your to-do list. That's okay. Let it go, for the serenity you achieve on most days will more than make up for it.

InPowering Meditation™

This technique came to me during one of my morning meditations. One of the benefits I've found from my practice is that I get inspired. I've received some of my best ideas while meditating, and although at first I may not know how to bring these thoughts to fruition, during this period of quiet focus, all the logistics fall into place.

This is what happened with InPowering Meditation. I felt that there were times I wanted to achieve a specific goal with my practice, be it changing a limiting belief or manifesting something I wanted to create in my life. How could I use meditation to help me reach my objective? While I pondered this, the word *InPowering* came to me; and before long, I'd put pen to paper and written all the thoughts I had about how this could work.

By combining journaling, affirmation creation, and guided meditation, I discovered that my morning practice took on a huge role in my manifesting skills. I was able to singularly focus on something I desired and create it or change a belief that no longer served me. Saying and thinking my affirmations throughout the day further enhanced the technique. Many wonderful things have come into my life due to this, and I'm currently teaching workshops on it across the country. It's truly one of my favorite things!

So THESE ARE MY SONGS . . . for now. Thanks so much for reading—that is, singing along. Even as I write this, I'm thinking of more tunes I'd like to share with you. Is there a sequel, perhaps? For now, though, I just want to remind you that we're all creating our songs each and every day, and they'll be remembered as representing who we are. It's not important if we're in tune or not. It's just important that we keep on singing!

⊞ ⊞ ⊞

Acknowledgments

We never walk alone, and that is so true with the writing of this book.

I'd like to thank Mark Husson, my agent, my mentor, and my friend; also Doreen Virtue, who gave me the confidence to know that I could accomplish anything. A thank-you to Cindy Pearlman, who helped me complete the book. We shared some wonderful laughs during the process. Thanks as well to all the wonderful people at Hay House, including Jessica Kelley, my editor, and Christy Salinas and her art department, who so captured the feeling of the book with the beautiful cover.

To all my friends who have supported me, encouraged me, and told me, "Yes, you can," when I truly felt that no, I couldn't: You were my superhero buddies who made me believe that I could leap a tall building in a single bound. You know who you are, and I say thank you to each and every one of you.

My family . . . well, where would I be without you, your love, and the marvelous adventures we've shared? Thanks for letting me be your mom, your sister, and your daughter.

And . . . drumroll please . . . a special thanks to my husband, Dennis. You never stopped believing in me and this project, even when my own beliefs wavered. We've shared many songs in this life together, and there's no one else I would choose to sing with than you.

❖ ❖ ❖

About the Author

Susan Dintino is an author, a motivational speaker, and a radio-show host who embraces the opportunity to reach out to a multitude of people in a way that blends humor with the life lessons she's learned along the way, speaking in locales as diverse as Kona, Hawaii, and Lily Dale, New York. As the host of the highly rated weekly radio show *Susan Dintino Live,* airing every Wednesday on **www.12radio.com**, Susan gets to the heart of the matter with her special brand of humor. Susan is also the author of the children's book *A Year of Me* and creator of the healing meditation CD *Butterfly Blessings.*

A trusted and popular advisor on **www.12listen.com**, Susan uses her intuitive abilities to provide her clients with clear guidance and advice that assists them in choosing the best path for their lives. *Susanisms* is a daily column on **www.12listen.com** that provides the readers with daily quips of motivation, inspiration, and sometimes a laugh or two. Susan keeps an active blog on her website **www.susandintino.com** that allows her to share her thoughts on everyday topics that bring chuckles and "Aha!" moments to her readers. She's also a proud contributor to many online magazines, including the popular **www.thirdage.com.**

Meditation is one of Susan's passions, and she's recently trademarked a new technique: InPowering Meditation™, which combines automatic writing, affirmation creation, and guided meditation to promote peace and serenity, as well as assisting listeners in manifesting what they desire.

Married for 40 years (Really?! Is that even possible or legal?), Susan is the mother of three daughters, has two sons-in-law, and is Nonni to three grandchildren with one on the way. A resident of Sanibel Island, Florida, she splits her time between the island and Buffalo, New York. Her hobbies include reading good books,

traveling, and staying out of the drama of her daughters' lives. Her motto is: "When the going gets tough, reach for the Ben & Jerry's Chunky Monkey!"

To find out more about Susan and her upcoming events, please visit **www.susandintino.com**.

⊞ ⊞ ⊞

Hay House Titles of Related Interest

YOU CAN HEAL YOUR LIFE, the movie, starring Louise L. Hay & Friends
(available as a 1-DVD program and an expanded 2-DVD set)
Watch the trailer at: **www.LouiseHayMovie.com**

THE SHIFT, the movie,
starring Dr. Wayne W. Dyer
(available as a 1-DVD program and an expanded 2-DVD set)
Watch the trailer at: **www.DyerMovie.com**

⊞

THE AGE OF MIRACLES: Embracing the New Midlife,
by Marianne Williamson

THE ANGEL THERAPY HANDBOOK, by Doreen Virtue

*THE ART OF EXTREME SELF-CARE: Transform Your Life One Month
at a Time,* by Cheryl Richardson

*CALM: A Proven Four-Step Process Designed Specifically for Women
Who Worry,* by Denise Marek

*JUICY LIVING, JUICY AGING: Kick Up Your Heels . . .
Before You're Too Short to Wear Them,* by Loretta LaRoche

*LOVESCOPES: What Astrology Knows About You
and the Ones You Love,* by Mark S. Husson

All of the above are available at your local bookstore,
or may be ordered by contacting Hay House (see next page).

⊞

We hope you enjoyed this Hay House Insights book.
If you'd like to receive our online catalog featuring additional
information on Hay House books and products, or if you'd like to
find out more about the Hay Foundation, please contact:

INSIGHTS

Hay House, Inc., P.O. Box 5100, Carlsbad, CA 92018-5100
(760) 431-7695 or (800) 654-5126
(760) 431-6948 (fax) or (800) 650-5115 (fax)
www.hayhouse.com® • **www.hayfoundation.org**

Published and distributed in Australia by: Hay House Australia
Pty. Ltd., 18/36 Ralph St., Alexandria NSW 2015 • *Phone:* 612-9669-4299
Fax: 612-9669-4144 • www.hayhouse.com.au

Published and distributed in the United Kingdom by: Hay House UK,
Ltd., 292B Kensal Rd., London W10 5BE • *Phone:* 44-20-8962-1230
Fax: 44-20-8962-1239 • www.hayhouse.co.uk

Published and distributed in the Republic of South Africa by:
Hay House SA (Pty), Ltd., P.O. Box 990, Witkoppen 2068
Phone/Fax: 27-11-467-8904 • www.hayhouse.co.za

Published in India by: Hay House Publishers India, Muskaan Complex,
Plot No. 3, B-2, Vasant Kunj, New Delhi 110 070 • *Phone:* 91-11-4176-1620
Fax: 91-11-4176-1630 • www.hayhouse.co.in

Distributed in Canada by: Raincoast, 9050 Shaughnessy St.,
Vancouver, B.C. V6P 6E5 • *Phone:* (604) 323-7100
Fax: (604) 323-2600 • www.raincoast.com

Take Your Soul on a Vacation

Visit **www.HealYourLife.com®** to regroup, recharge, and reconnect
with your own magnificence. Featuring blogs, mind-body-spirit
news, and life-changing wisdom from Louise Hay and friends.

Visit **www.HealYourLife.com** today!

Free Mind-Body-Spirit e-Newsletters

From Hay House, the Ultimate Resource for Inspiration

Be the first to know about Hay House's dollar deals, free downloads, special offers, affirmation cards, giveaways, contests, and more!

 Get exclusive excerpts from our latest releases and videos from *Hay House Present Moments*.

 Enjoy uplifting personal stories, how-to articles, and healing advice, along with videos and empowering quotes, within *Heal Your Life*.

 Have an inspirational story to tell and a passion for writing? Sharpen your writing skills with insider tips from *Your Writing Life*.

Receive uplifting affirmations, empowering thoughts, and healing wisdom from *Louise Hay*.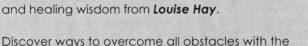

Discover ways to overcome all obstacles with the inspiring words of *Dr. Wayne Dyer* to get your wishes fulfilled.

Get angelic, heavenly assistance for your everyday life from angel expert and lifelong clairvoyant *Doreen Virtue*.

Uncover the timeless secrets of life from *Gregg Braden* and discover the collective wisdom of our past.

Get inspired, educate yourself, and share the wisdom!
Visit www.hayhouse.com to sign up today!

 HAY HOUSE

 HAYHOUSE RADIO
radio for your soul

HealYourLife.com

Heal Your Life One Thought at a Time . . .
on Louise's All-New Website!

"Life is bringing me everything I need and more."

— Louise Hay

Come to HEALYOURLIFE.COM today and meet the world's best-selling self-help authors; the most popular leading intuitive, health, and success experts; up-and-coming inspirational writers; and new like-minded friends who will share their insights, experiences, personal stories, and wisdom so you can heal your life and the world around you . . . one thought at a time.

Here are just some of the things you'll get at HealYourLife.com:

- DAILY AFFIRMATIONS
- CAPTIVATING VIDEO CLIPS
- EXCLUSIVE BOOK REVIEWS
- AUTHOR BLOGS
- LIVE TWITTER AND FACEBOOK FEEDS
- BEHIND-THE-SCENES SCOOPS
- LIVE STREAMING RADIO
- "MY LIFE" COMMUNITY OF FRIENDS

PLUS:
FREE Monthly Contests and Polls
FREE BONUS gifts, discounts,
and newsletters

Make It Your Home Page Today!
www.HealYourLife.com®

HEAL YOUR LIFE®

Lightning Source UK Ltd.
Milton Keynes UK
UKOW050646070612

193938UK00001B/23/P